T0372272

FUNGAL INSPIRATION

Published and distributed by
viction:workshop ltd.

viction:ary™

viction:workshop ltd.
Unit C, 7/F, Seabright Plaza,
9-23 Shell Street, North Point, Hong Kong SAR
Website: www.victionary.com
Email: we@victionary.com
@victionworkshop
@victionworkshop
Bē @victionary
@victionary

Edited & produced by viction:ary

Creative direction by Victor Cheung
Book design by viction:workshop ltd.
Showcase & quote typeface: Ogg by Sharp Type
Cover illustrations by James Barker, Rhian Davie Illustration, Rita Gould, and Sundra Art
Endpaper image: Mushroom Forest by Selcha Uni

Second Edition

ISBN 978-988-75666-1-8
Printed and bound in China

FUNGAL INSPIRATION

ART AND ILLUSTRATION INSPIRED BY WILD NATURE

PREFACE

BY VICTION:ARY

What comes to mind when you think of nature? Is it sunlight filtering through the leaves atop a lush forest, fresh flowers in a garden, or fruits and berries hanging off their branches? Needless to say, Mother Nature is plentiful when it comes to creating these beauties. However, have you ever wondered what silently thrives in the shadows or beneath the loam?

Having published a number of nature-related books including Flora & Fauna and Botanical Inspiration, we were more than compelled to add to the collection by following up with an illustration book solely about the mystical family of fungi, which are equally as fascinating as the botanical wonders that live above the ground. Often mistaken as a plant, mushrooms are actually fruiting bodies of a fungus, and belong in their own unique category alongside plants and animals. That is to say, the fungi family is perhaps one of the most fascinating species that Earth has to offer.

Hidden in damp corners and lichen-covered spots out of the sun, mushrooms and toadstools are often regarded to be shrouded in mystery. While some are poisonous and some are gathered by humans for their edible or psychoactive properties, these curious saprophytes also make appearances in folklore and fairytales, the most notable mentions being the magic mushrooms which Alice eats on her journey to Wonderland. This comes to show that not only are fungi indispensable for the Earth's ecosystem and for our nourishment, but they also feed our creativity in fantasy literature and art with their charming and mysterious qualities.

In Fungal Inspiration, you will find various interpretations of the mycolic world created by illustrators and artists from around the globe.

Some illustrators such as Martha Iserman (PP. 006-009) set out to replicate each mushroom's details and forms with precise, botanical accuracy. reminiscent of those found in scientific records. Similarly, Song Kang (PP. 010-019) also gives prominence to the details, but with a more vibrant palette with overlapping watercolour hues.

One may also find themselves enchanted by the whimsical collages of Amy Ross (PP. 082-089), where she juxtaposes fungi with human torsos, and combines snippets from vintage and Renaissance portraits to create weird but wonderful mushroom people with distinct personalities and donning garbs of all sorts. Known for her mesmerising depictions of dream scenarios, Fuco Ueda (PP. 128-135) also incorporates mushrooms into her world of ennui-faced girls with a slightly darker and haunting touch.

For works that truly incorporate the magical and fantastical elements of fairytales, L&W Studio (PP. 276-283) weaves toadstool-covered dream-scapes in psychedelic colours, where one with an observant eye would be able to decipher the story happening within. On the other hand, Léa Chaillaud (PP. 226-233) also creates endearing and light-hearted portraits of mushrooms and toadstools fused into the fauna of the lands, transforming ordinary creatures into charming works of art.

Dedicated to celebrating the lesser-known side of the natural world, Fungal Inspiration serves to bring out the rich diversity of these often overlooked but crucial driving forces on our planet. Moreover, it shows that inspiration often lies in the most unexpected places, and all it takes is just a little more digging to find it.

MARTHA ISERMAN

SONG KANG

CLAIRE BURBRIDGE

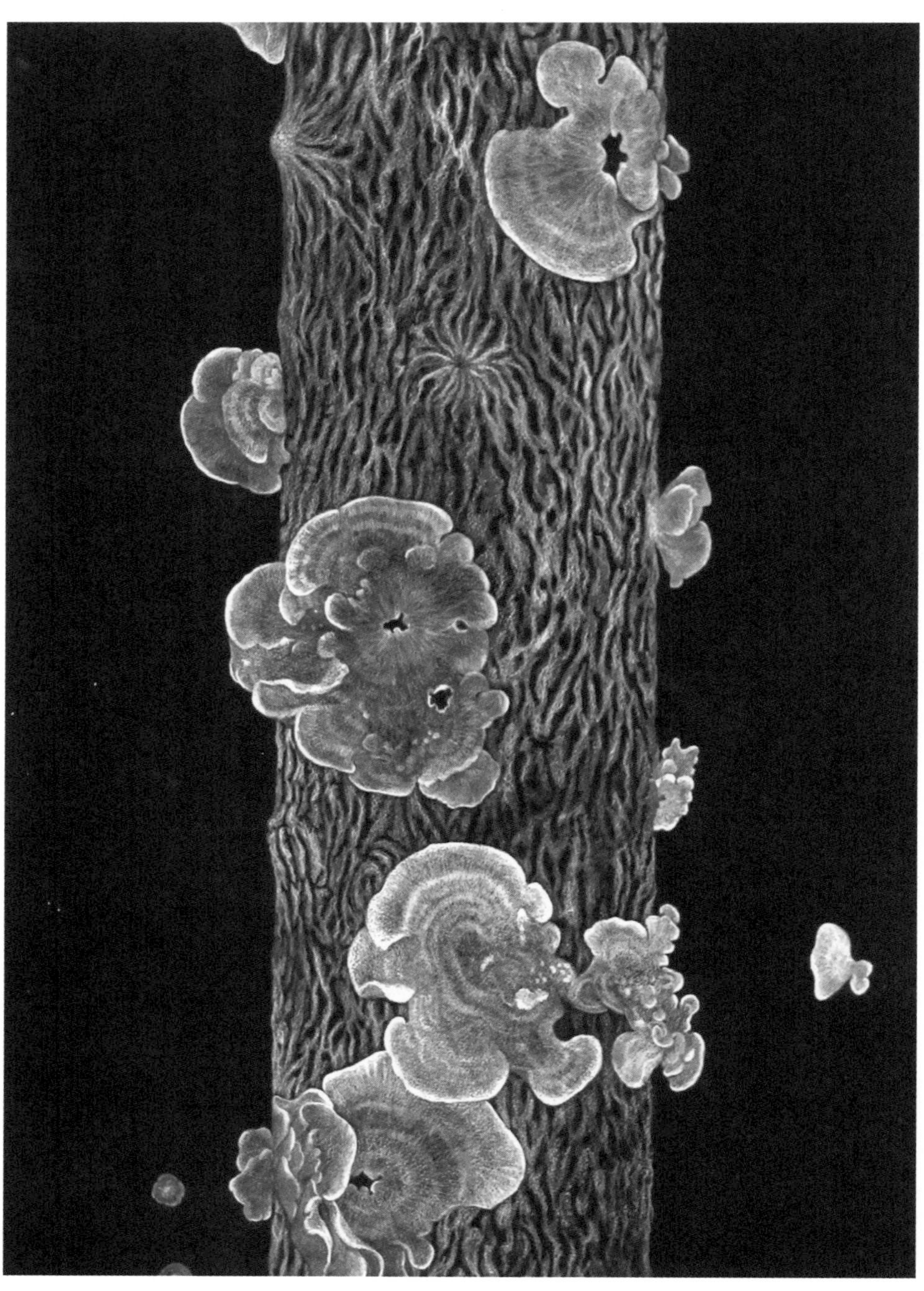

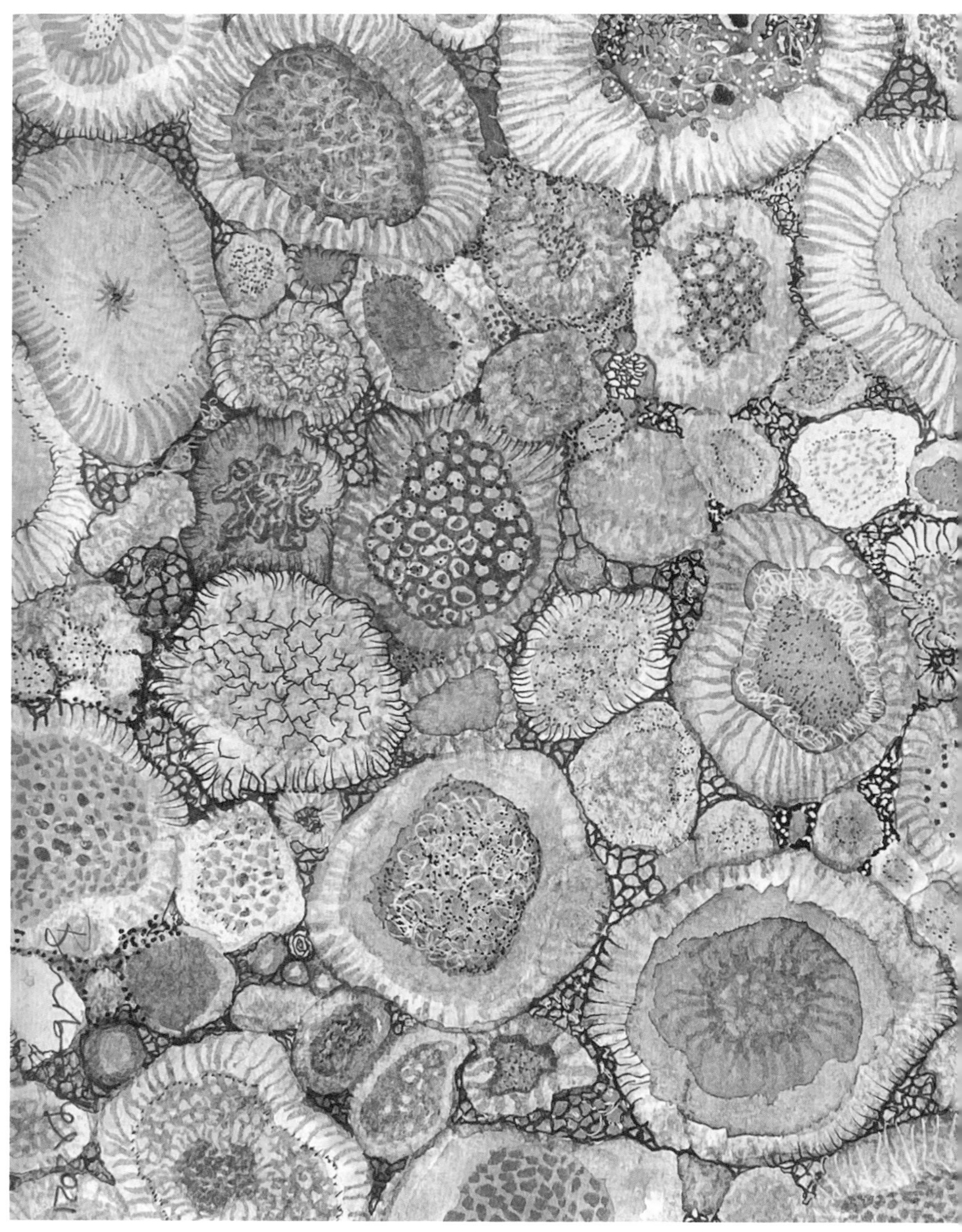

Those who know
walk out to gather, choosing
the benign from flocks
of glitterers, sorcerers,
russulas,
panther caps,
shark-white death angels
in their town veils
looking innocent as sugar
but full of paralysis:
to eat
is to stagger down
fast as mushrooms themselves
when they are done being perfect
and overnight
slide back under the shining
fields of rain.

Excerpt from 'Mushrooms'
by Mary Oliver

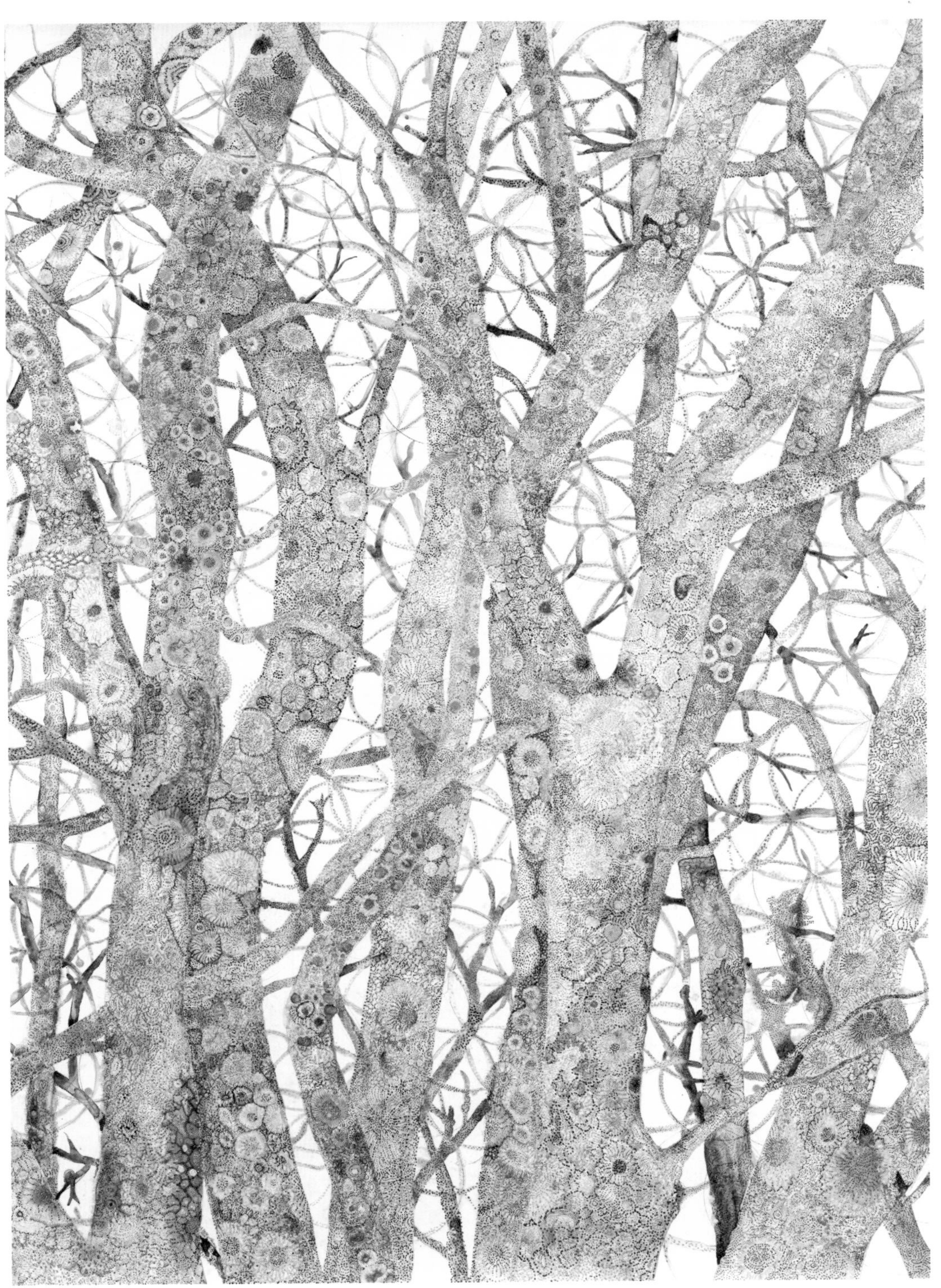

AMANDA SCHUTZ

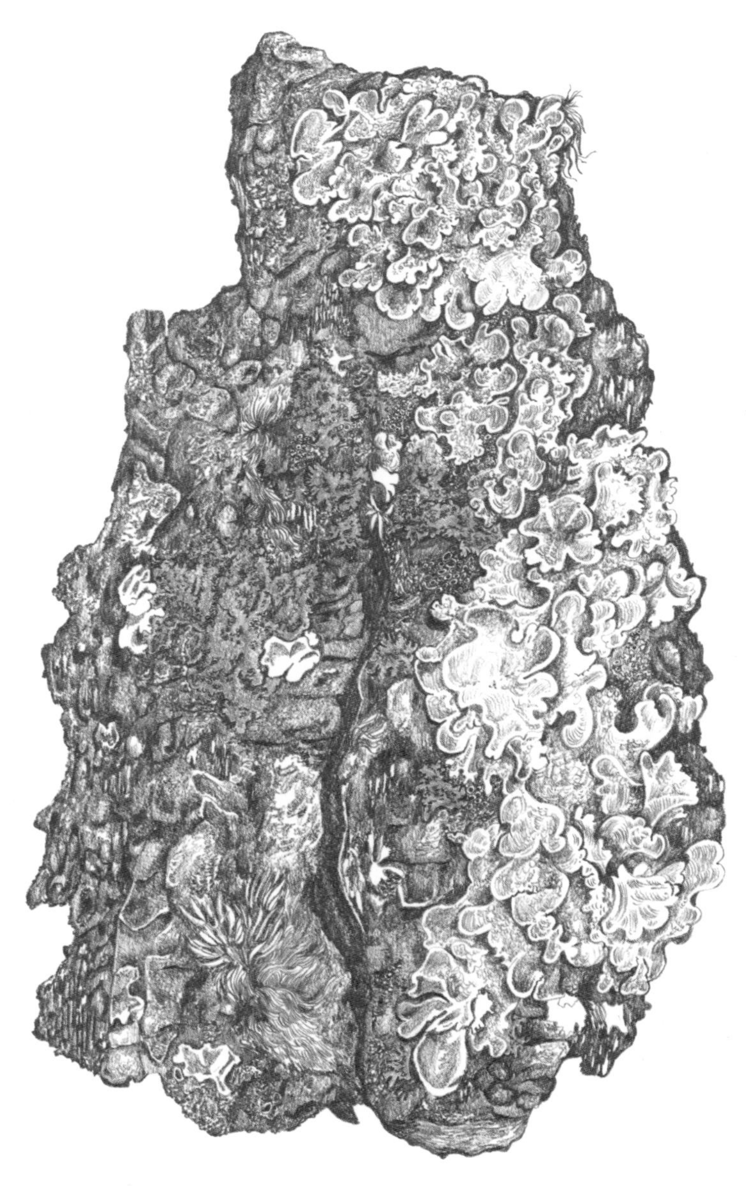

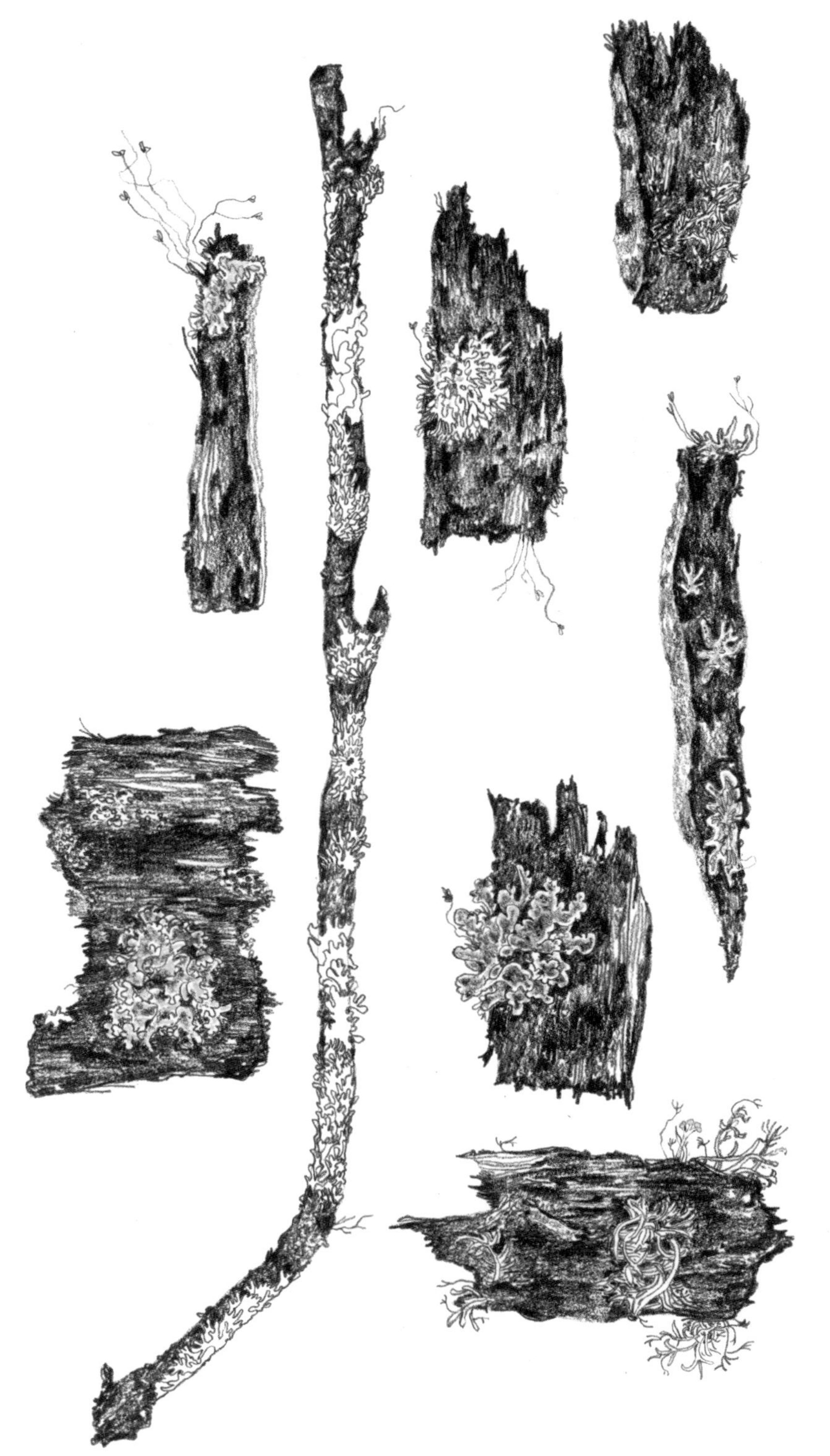

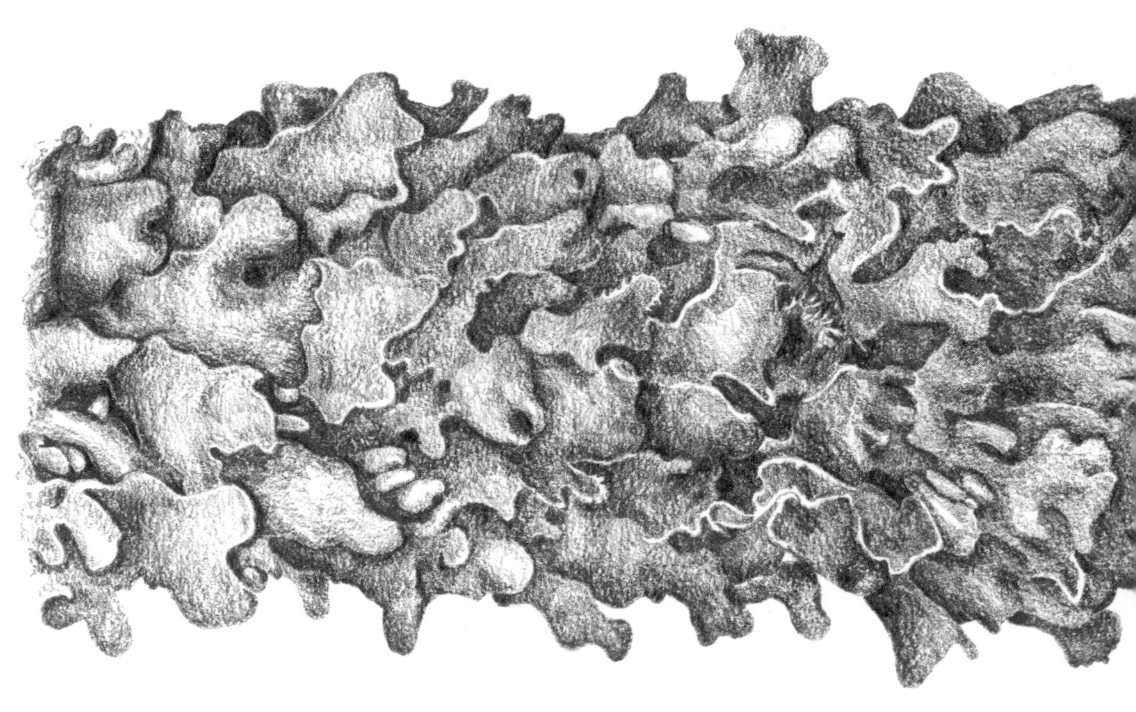

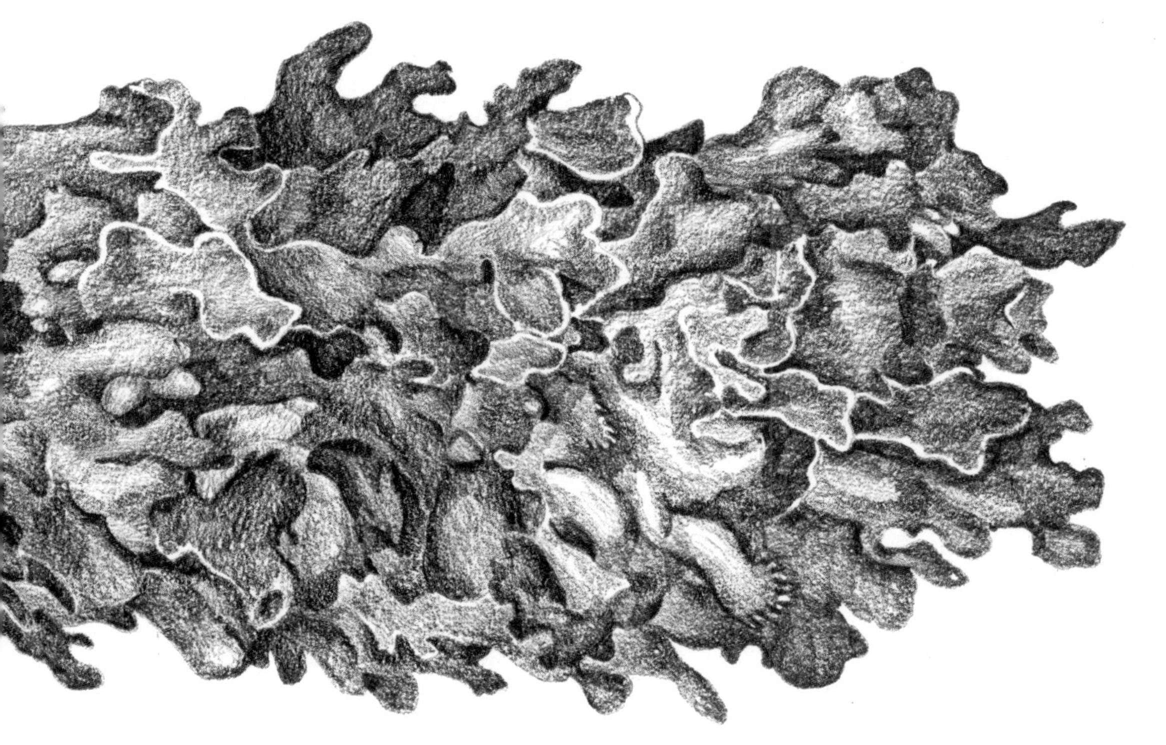

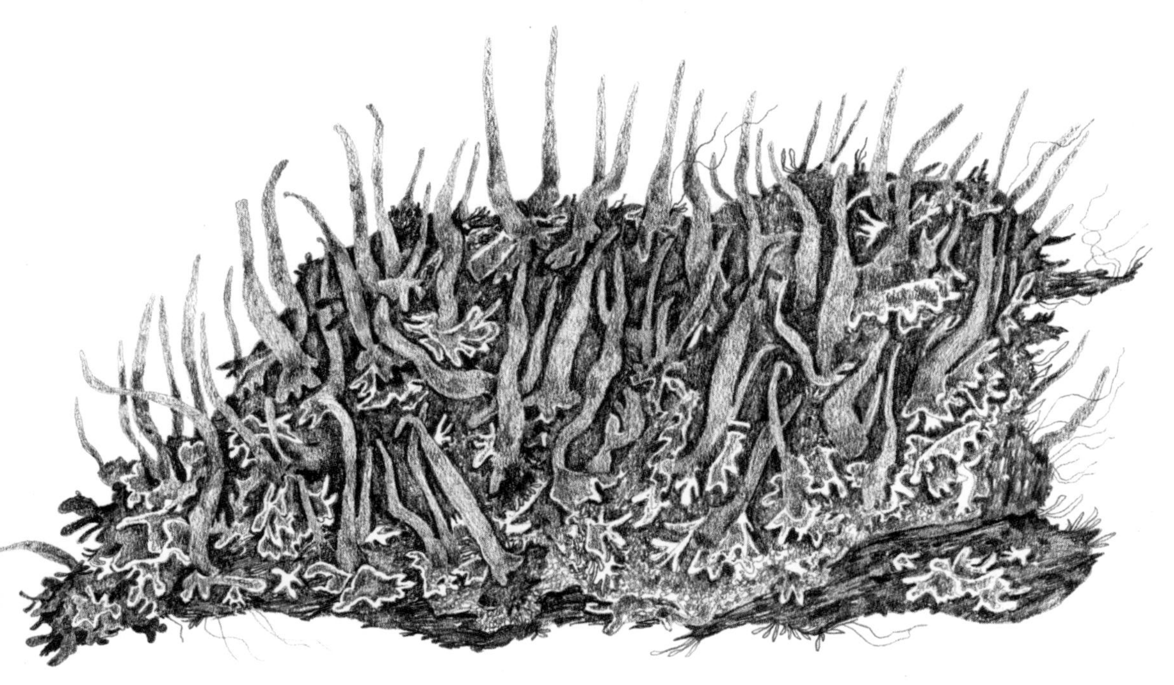

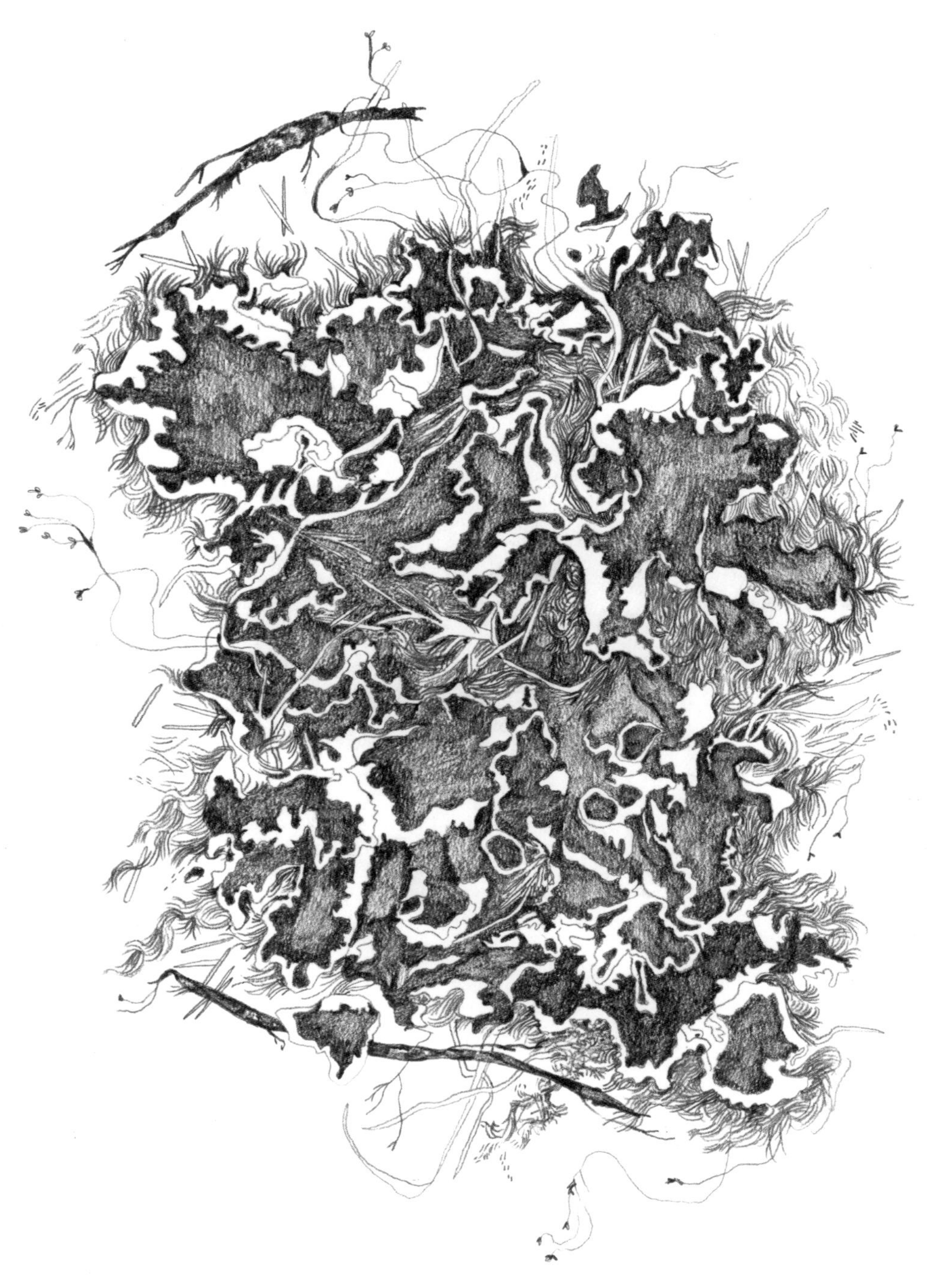

KIRRILY ANDERSON

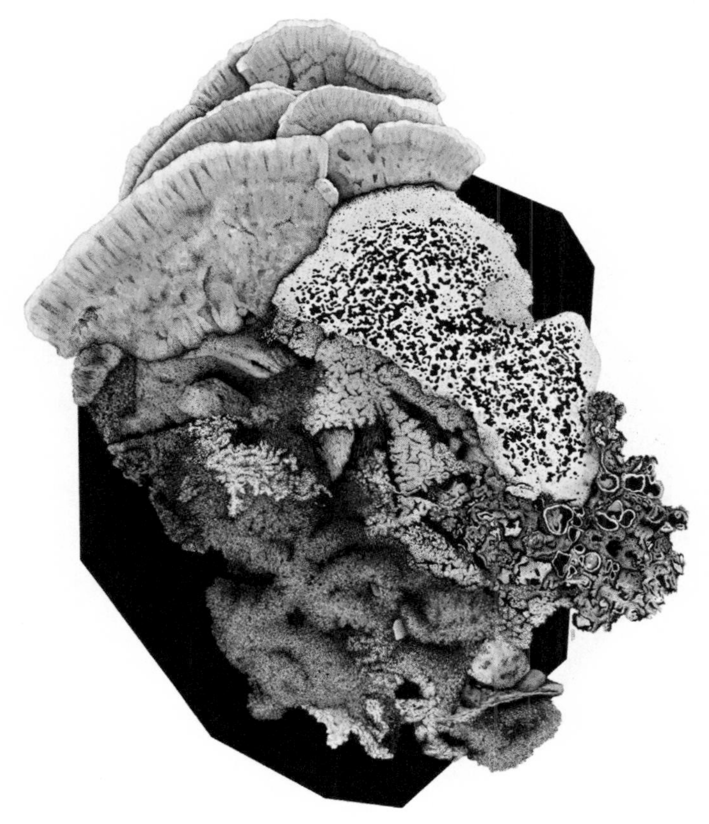

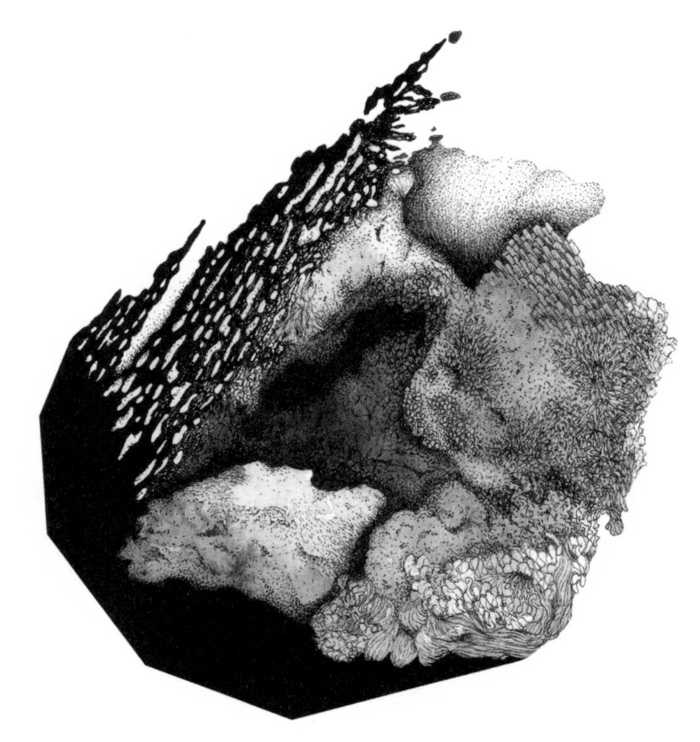

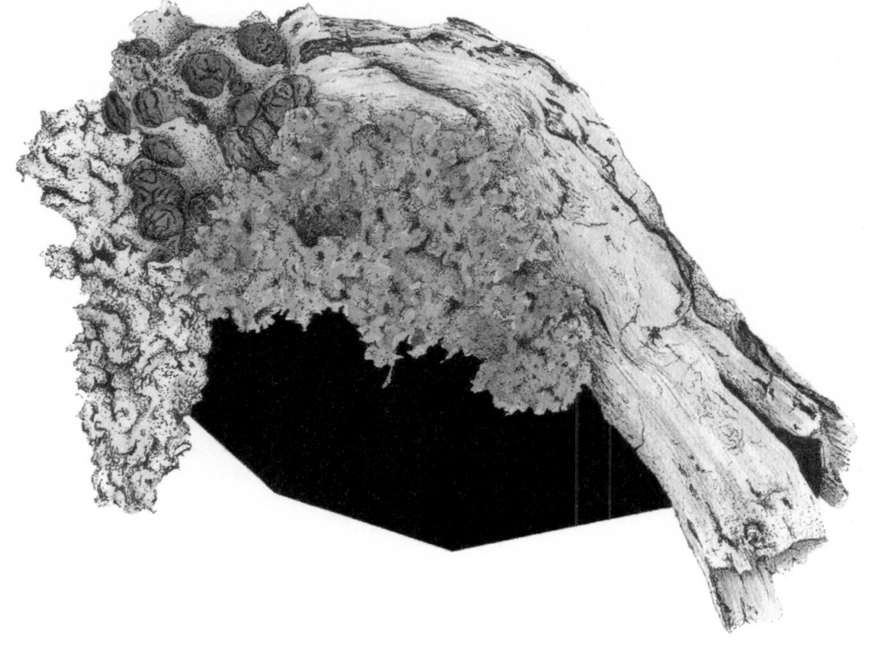

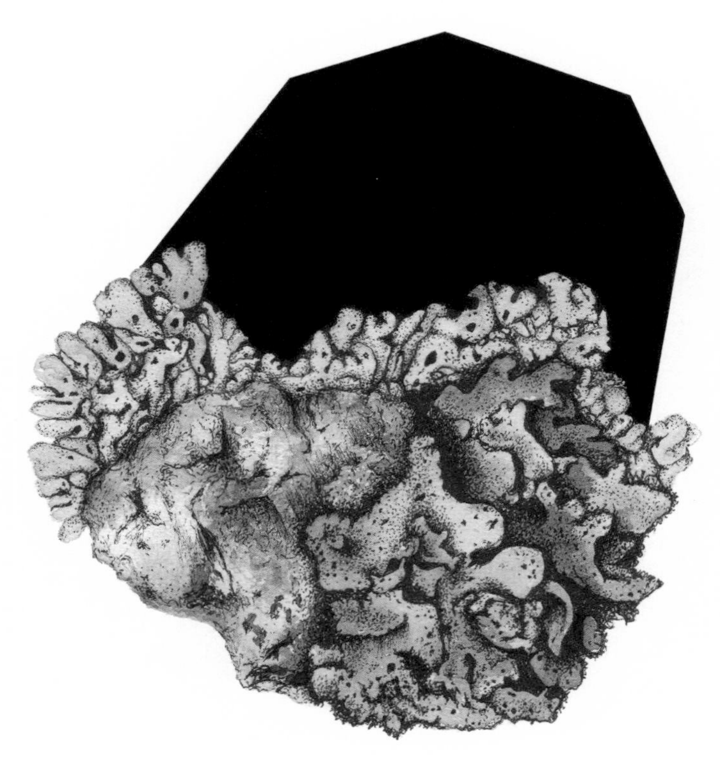

HOLDZELINE

POLA HEREDIA

ELENA ANDRONOVA

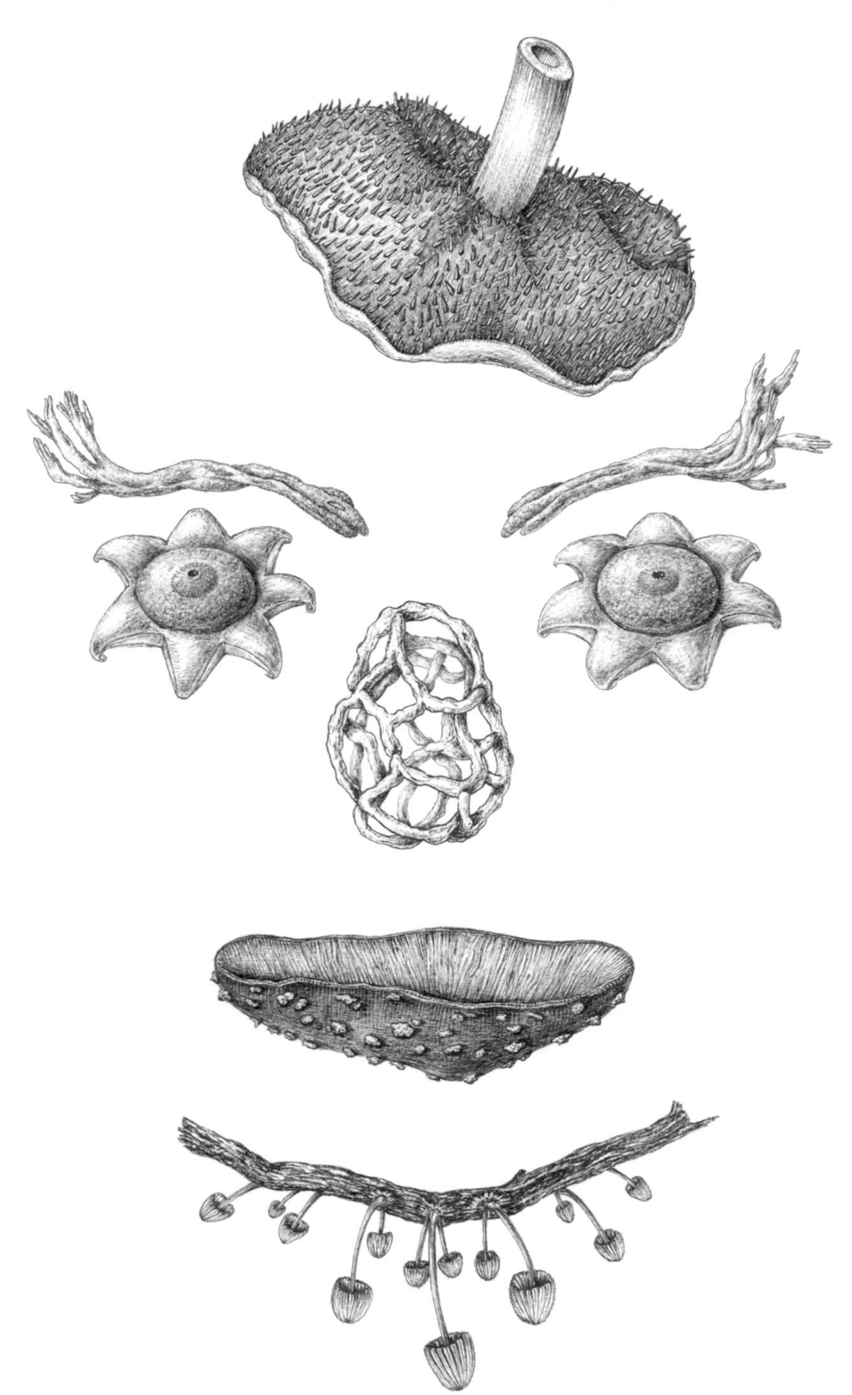

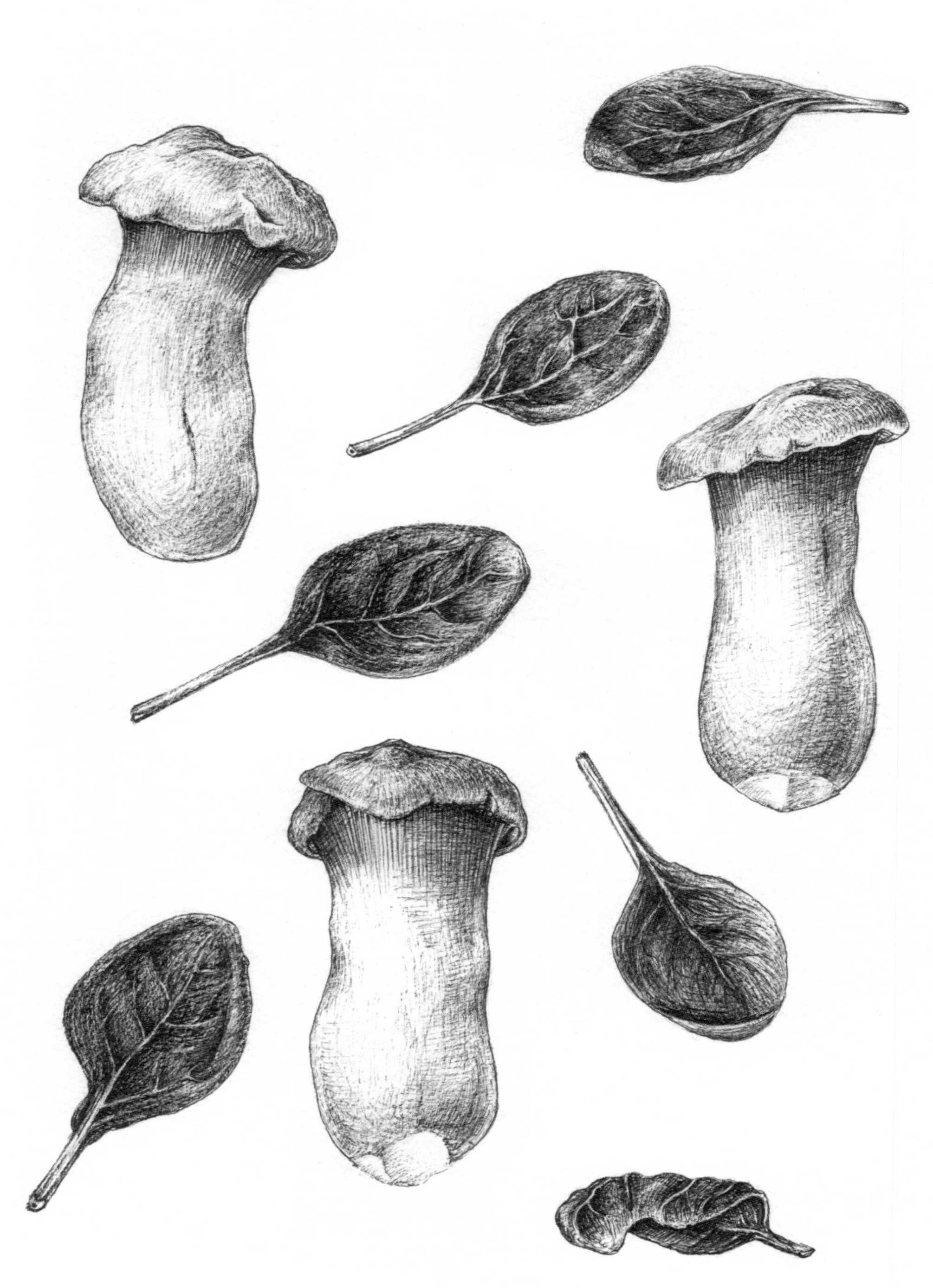

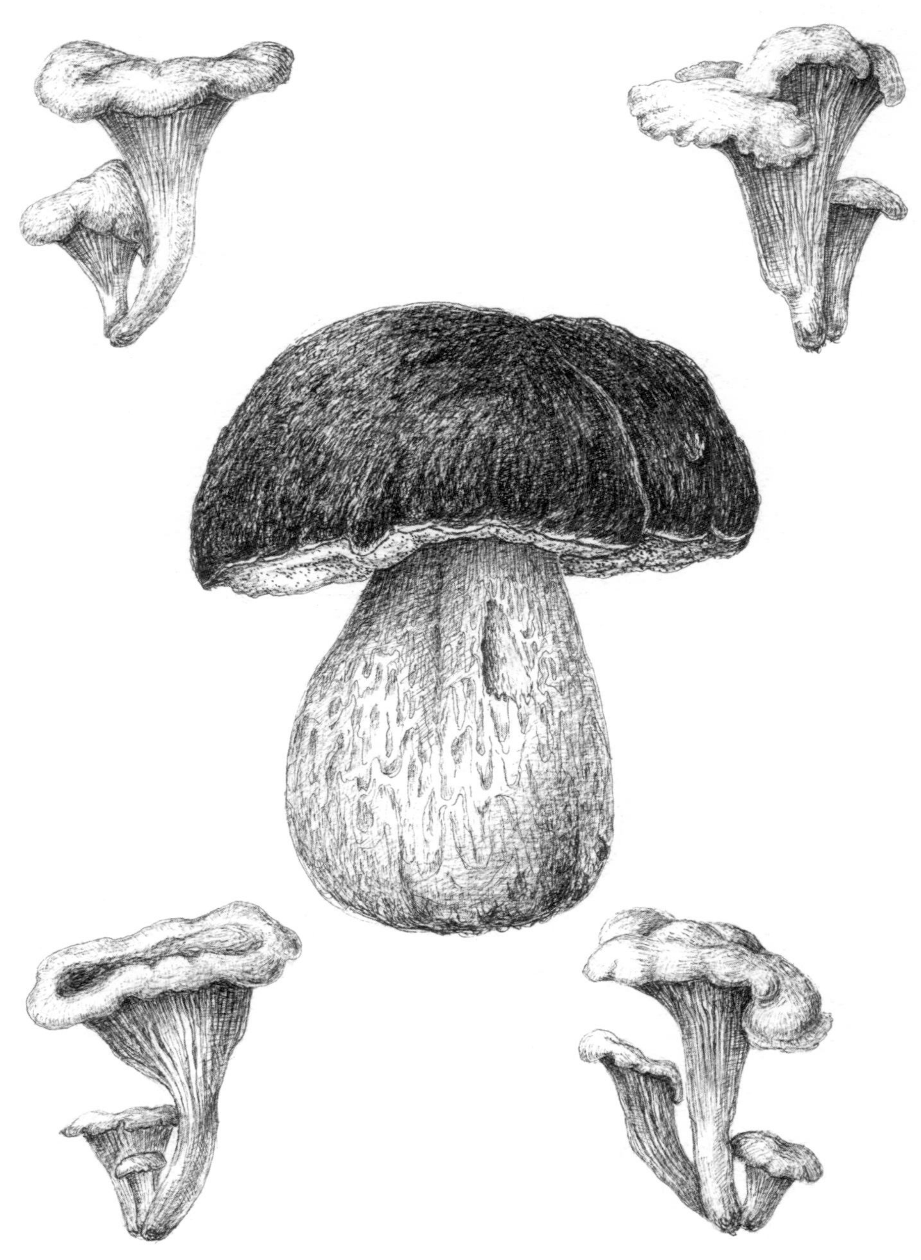

JOHN CASEY

MARTHA ISERMAN

bigredsharks.com

Martha is an Australian science illustrator and watercolour artist. She's most interested in creating unique biological worlds by depicting familiar organisms in unfamiliar ways. Her painting style is very detailed, using colour, composition, and form to break out of traditional representational art tropes.

006 AMBERGRIS #2
Watercolours, Paper
700 x 530 mm

007 AMBERGRIS #3
Watercolours, Paper
700 x 530 mm

008 MUSHROOMS
Watercolours, Paper
700 x 530 mm

009 AMBERGRIS #1
Watercolours, Paper
700 x 530 mm

SONG KANG

song-kang.com

Song Kang is a Korean-American freelance illustrator based in Atlanta, Georgia. Kang creates intricately rendered environments in pen and ink, drawing the commonplace flora, grass, mushrooms, and leaves and weaving them into new, fantastical worlds. While the majority of her illustrations are drawn in ink, Kang also incorporates a wide range of painting mediums and drawing tools in her practice, stretching the limits of how ink can be utilised as a traditional medium.

010 SPORE
Ink, Paper, Digital
457 x 457 mm

011 SHROOMS
Pen, Ink, Paper
153 x 203 mm

012 OYSTER MUSHROOM & PILLAR CORAL (From the "Land Corals" series)
Ink, Paper
230 x 230 mm

013 INDIGO MILK CAP & BIPINNATE SEA PLUME (From the "Land Corals" series)
Ink, Paper
230 x 230 mm

014 WEREWERE-KOKAKO & VENUS FAN (From the "Land Corals" series)
Ink, Paper
230 x 230 mm

015 FLY AGARIC & DISC CORAL (From the "Land Corals" series)
Ink, Paper
230 x 230 mm

016 TURKEY TAIL & ORGAN PIPE CORAL (From the "Land Corals" series)
Ink, Paper
230 x 230 mm

017 FUNGICULTURE
Ink, Paper
203 x 254 mm

018 / 019 EVOLUTION OF PLANTS
Pen, Ink, Paper
762 x 508 mm

CLAIRE BURBRIDGE

claireburbridge.com

Born in London, Claire studied Fine Art and History of Art at Oxford University and received her Masters from Camberwell College of Art. In 2010, she moved to Oregon beginning a deep study of nature, creating complex large-scale works on paper. Her works are in public and private collections worldwide. She has also designed a range of custom-made eco-friendly wallpapers.

020 SIRENS 2
Pen, Ink, Watercolours
781 x 1060 mm

021 THE NOCTURNAL LIFE OF TREES 2
Pen, Ink, Watercolours, Wax Pigment Pencil
1778 x 1143 mm

022 LISTENING TREE 2
Graphite, Wax Pigment Colour Pencil
711 x 533 mm

023 LISTENING TREE 1
Wax Pigment Pencil, White Indian Ink
711 x 533 mm

024 / 025 MIDSUMMER LICHEN STUDY
Pen, Ink, Watercolours
304 x 241 mm

027 UNIFIED FIELD 2
Pen, Ink, Natural Pigment Watercolours, Sodium Crystals, Yupo
1524 x 1498 mm

AMANDA SCHUTZ

amandaschutz.com

As the founder and creator of Curio Studio, Amanda Schutz has carefully cultivated a successful design business for over 20 years. Amanda has taught design & illustration at MacEwan University, is past Albertan president of Graphic Designers of Canada, and in 2022 was named a Fellow of the Design Professionals of Canada. All featured artworks are funded by the Edmonton Arts Council

028 XANTHOMENDOZA FALLAX
(Hooded Sunburst)
Pencil, Pencil Crayon, Paper
432 x 228 mm

029 PHYSCIA STELLARIS
(Grey Star)
Pencil, Pencil Crayon, Paper
254 x 305 mm

030 VULPICIDA PINASTRI
(Powdered Sunshine)
Pencil, Pencil Crayon, Paper
203 x 279 mm

031 PARMELIA SULCATA
(Hammered Shield)
Pencil, Pencil Crayon, Paper
229 x 279 mm

032 / 033 HYPOGYMNIA PHYSODES
(Hooded Tube)
Pencil, Pencil Crayon, Paper
482 x 140 mm

034 PHYSCIA ADSCENDENS
(Hooded Rosette)
Pencil, Pencil Crayon, Paper
178 x 203 mm

035 CLADONIA CONIOCRAEA
(Common Powderhorn)
Pencil, Pencil Crayon, Paper
254 x 152 mm

036 PELTIGERA
(Concentric Pelt)
Pencil, Pencil Crayon, Paper
279 x 229 mm

037 USNEA
(Old Man's Beard)
Pencil, Pencil Crayon, Paper
584 x 305 mm

KIRRILY ANDERSON
kirrilyanderson.com

Australian artist Kirrily Anderson is inspired by the small details of nature — whether illustrated in delicate ink and watercolours on paper, or as public murals. Moving from Melbourne to regional Victoria in 2017 encouraged a change in style, focusing on nature, particularly as the subject of murals, of which she has painted more than 20 since 2018.

038 FOREST III
Ink, Watercolours, Paper
360 x 460 mm

039 EXQUISITE GROWTH
Ink, Watercolours, Paper
560 x 655 mm

040 FOREST I
Ink, Watercolours, Paper
200 x 200 mm

041 PRETTY VALLEY
Ink, Watercolours, Paper
290 x 265 mm

042 CATANI
Ink, Watercolours, Paper
115 x 115 mm

043 ROCKY VALLEY DAM
Ink, Watercolours, Paper
300 x 300 mm

HOLDZELINE
holdzeline.com

Holdzeline, or Tamara Thys uses Indian ink, dots, and with a lots of detail to create graphic botanical illustrations. By playing with shadows, framing or scales, she seeks to highlight details, textures, and particular shapes that can be found in nature.

044 POLYPORUS ALVEOLARIS
Black Ink
210 x 297 mm

045 CHAMPIGNONS, MOUVEMENT
Black Ink
210 x 297 mm

046 BOLETUS
Black Ink
210 x 297 mm

047 AMANITE 2
Black Ink
210 x 297 mm

048 AMANITE
Black Ink
210 x 297 mm

049 COULEMELLE
Black Ink
210 x 297 mm

POLA HEREDIA
instagram.com/callampoli.art

Pola is a Chilean illustrator and graphic designer based in Santiago, California. With a deep love for everything fungi, she believes that her work can give this Queendom visibility and a voice.

050 CANTHERELLUS CIBARIUS (Fungi Foundation)
Tachikawa Maru Mapping Pen, Archival Ink
100 x 70 mm

051 MUSHROOM CLUSTER
0.1 Sakura Micron Fineliner
120 x 100 mm

052 FLAMMULINA SP.
0.1 Sakura Micron Fineliner
150 x 150 mm

053 BODY OF MOTHER
0.1 Sakura Micron Fineliner
150 mm x 100 mm

ELENA ANDRONOVA

instagram.com/elenaandronovaart

Born in Moscow, Elena is known for her intricately-detailed ink drawings of nature, which merge classical and graphic art influences. Previously a mathematician, her love of art inspired her to found an art gallery in 1999. Having studied at the Andriaka Academy, she was recognised for her singular graphical style and mathematical precision. Elena has exhibited in a number of group and solo exhibitions, and works under the social handle @elenaandronovaart.

054 MAMA SHROOM
Ink, Watercolour Paper
420 x 300 mm

055 SHROOM FACE
Ink, Watercolour Paper
600 x 420 mm

056 HONEY MUSHROOMS
Ink, Watercolour Paper
420 x 300 mm

057 OYSTER MUSHROOMS
Ink, Watercolour Paper
420 x 300 mm

058 ERYNGII AND SPINACH LEAVES
Ink, Watercolour Paper
420 x 300 mm

059 CEP AND CHANTERELLES
Ink, Watercolour Paper
420 x 300 mm

JOHN CASEY

johncasey.com

Born on Friday the 13th in Salem, John Casey started inventing creatures as a child. He is fascinated with skulls, teeth, spirographic eyes, and invented body parts, and often introduces anthropomorphic flora and fauna to his drawings, paintings, and sculptures. John graduated from the Massachusetts College of Art with a BFA and currently lives in California with his wife, artist Mary Kalin-Casey.

060 CAPRA FLY MUSCARIA
Pencil, Colour Pencil, Paper
355.6 x 279.4 mm

061 GOAT SHAMAN
Pencil, Colour Pencil, Paper
355.6 x 279.4 mm

062 MUSHROOM LOVE
Pencil, Colour Pencil, Paper
355.6 x 279.4 mm

063 THESE TWO
Pencil, Colour Pencil, Paper
355.6 x 279.4 mm

064 PINK MUSH
Pencil, Colour Pencil, Paper
355.6 x 279.4 mm

065 WAREWARE-KOKAKO
Pencil, Colour Pencil, Paper
355.6 x 279.4 mm

066 PUFF 'N' JEFF
Pencil, Colour Pencil, Paper
330.2 x 381 mm

067 CROSSED PAIRS
Pencil, Colour Pencil, Paper
355.6 x 279.4 mm

068 FANBOY
Pencil, Colour Pencil, Paper
355.6 x 279.4 mm

069 OLD FLAME
Pencil, Colour Pencil, Paper
355.6 x 279.4 mm

BECCA BOYCE

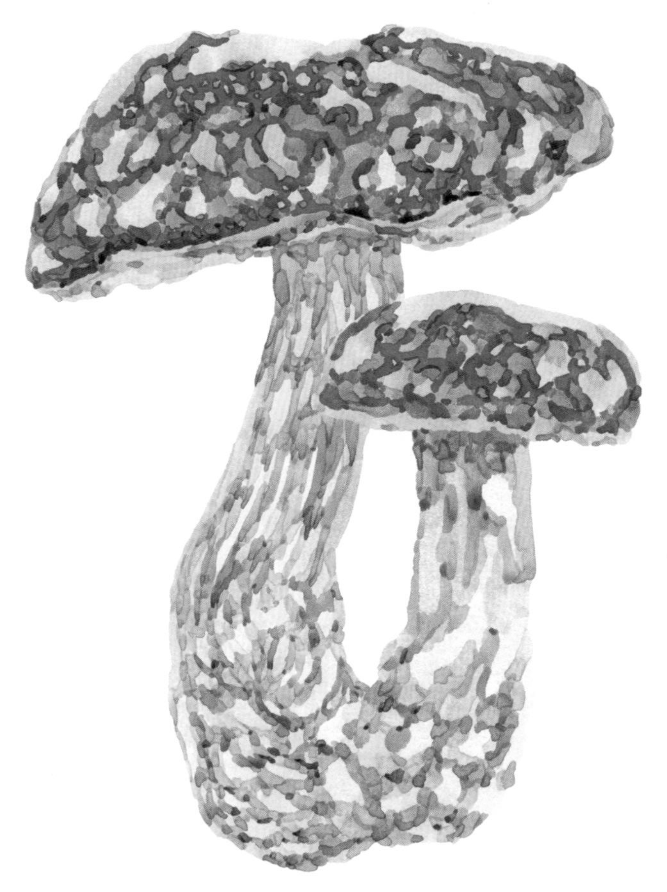

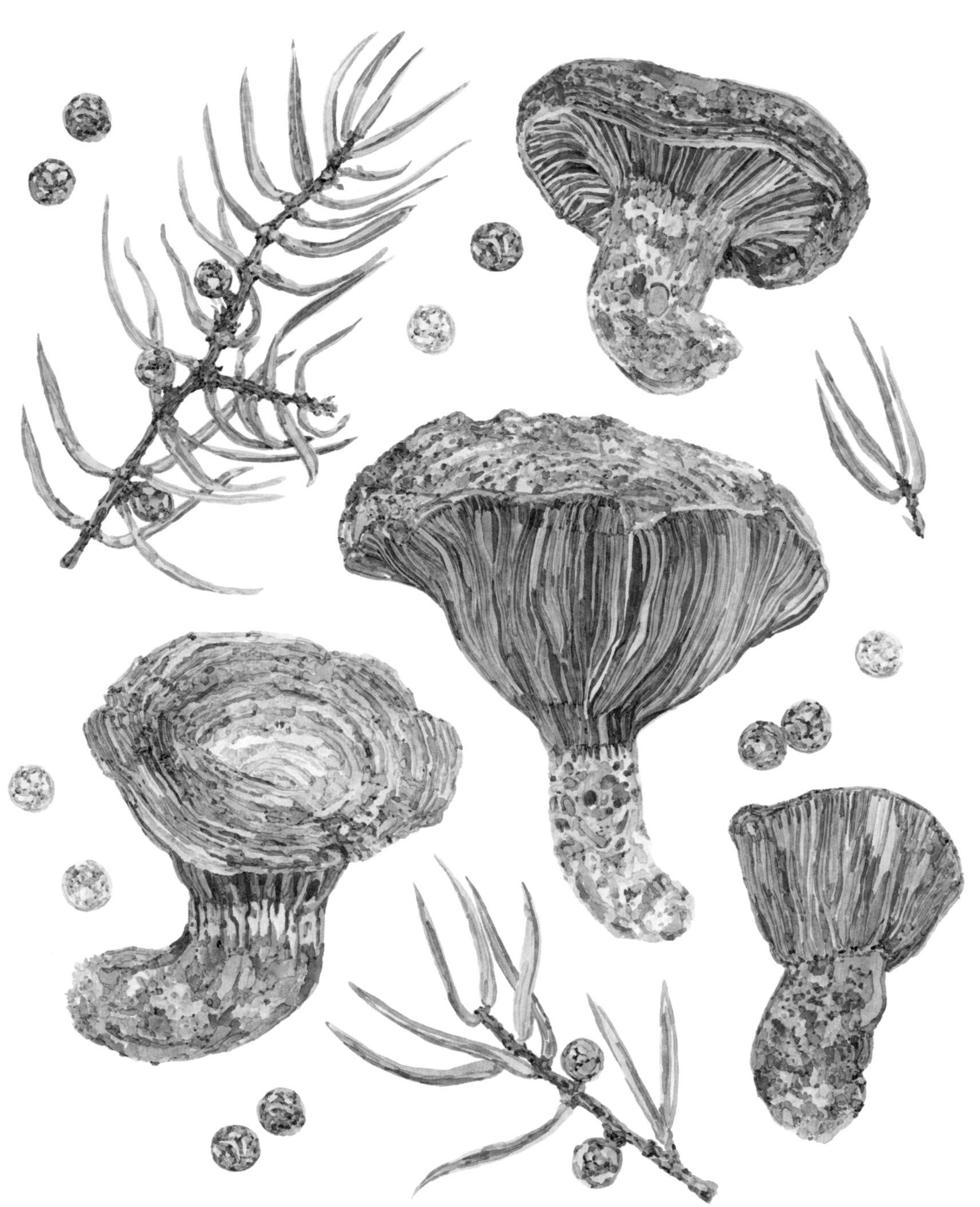

AMY ROSS

CECI LAM

ceci

ceci

ceci

HOME
SWEET
HOME

DEANNE CHEUK

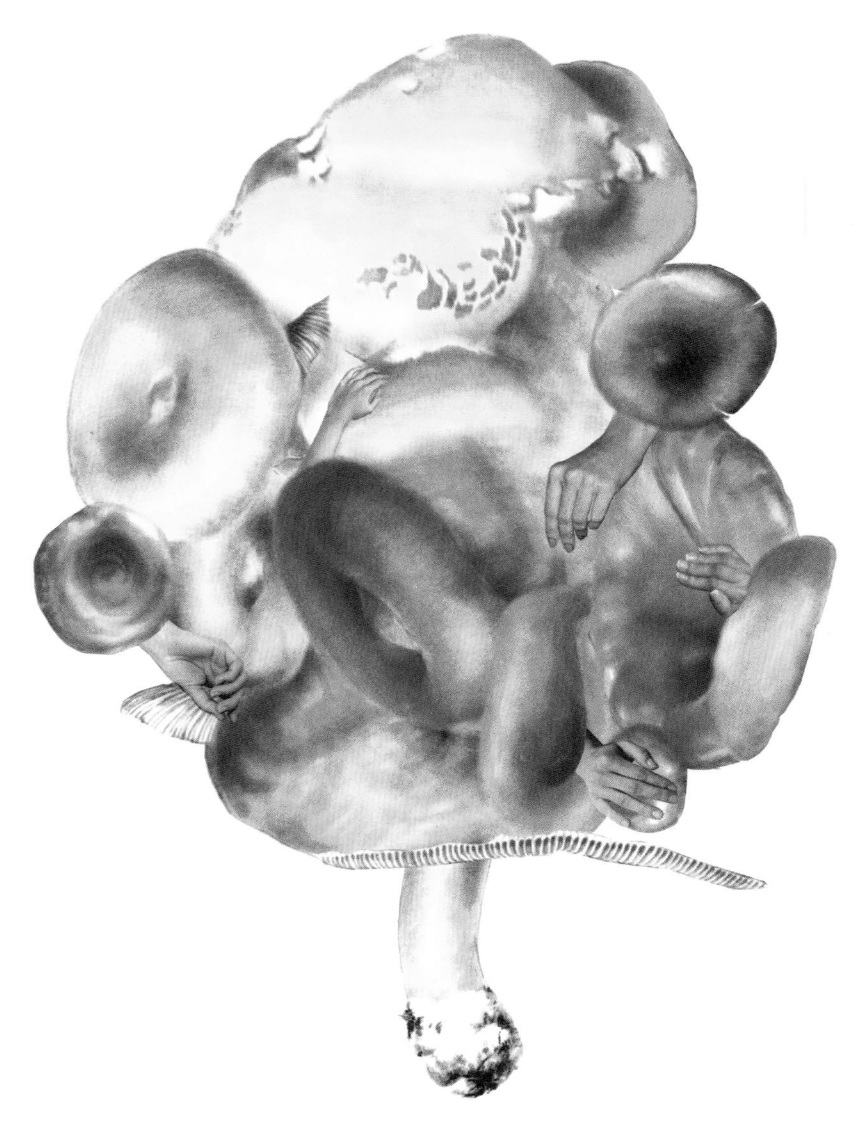

JIAYUE LI

The Mushroom is the Elf of Plants
At Evening, it is not
At Morning, in a Truffled Hut
It stop upon a Spot
As if it tarried always
And yet its whole Career
Is shorter than a Snake's Delay
And fleeter than a Tare
'Tis Vegetation's Juggler
The Germ of Alibi
Doth like a Bubble antedate
And like a Bubble, hie
I feel as if the Grass was pleased
To have it intermit
This surreptitious scion
Of Summer's circumspect.
Had Nature any supple Face
Or could she one contemn
Had Nature an Apostate
That Mushroom — it is Him!

'The Mushroom is the Elf of Plants'
by Emily Dickinson

EMMA BLACK

E Black-20

FUCO UEDA

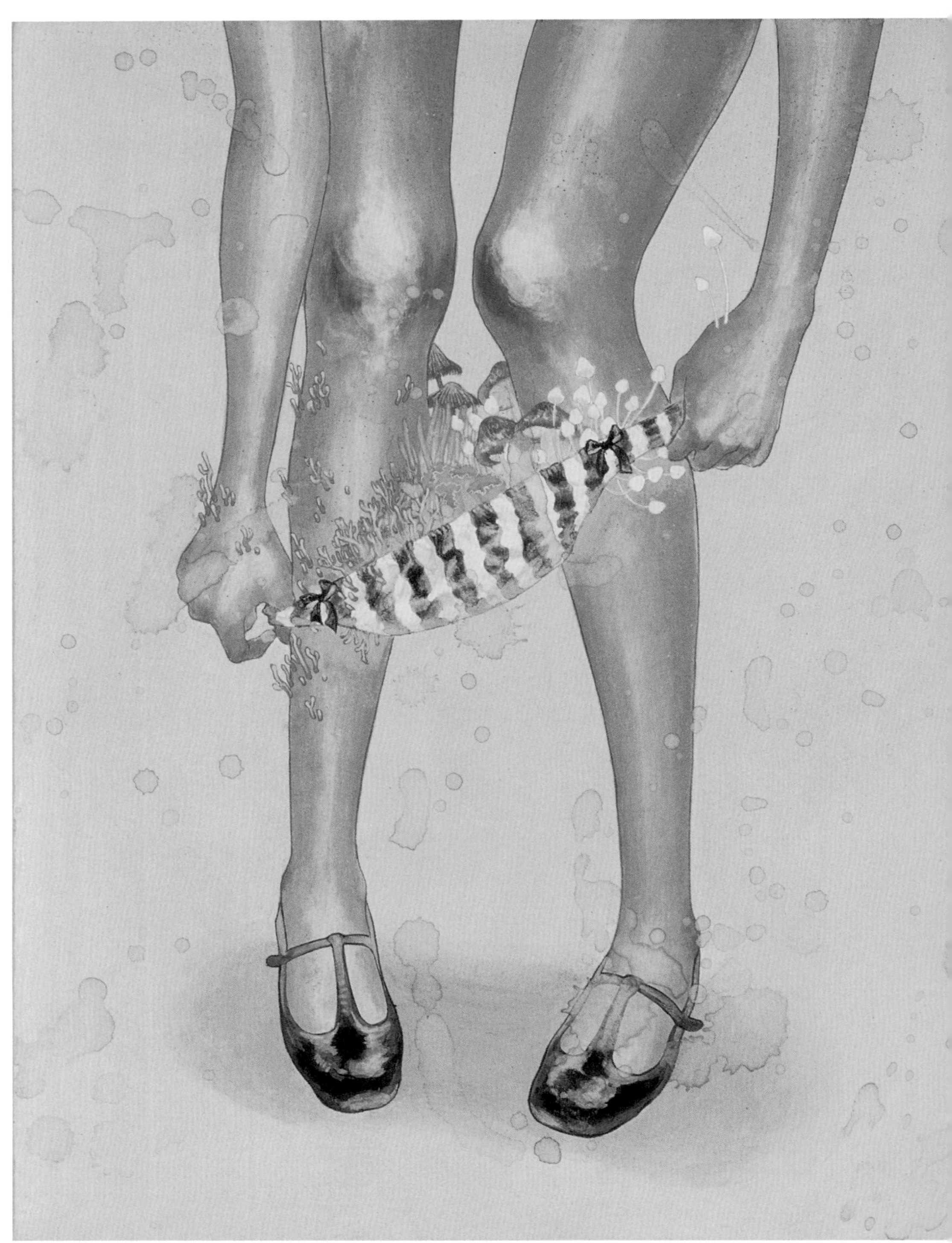

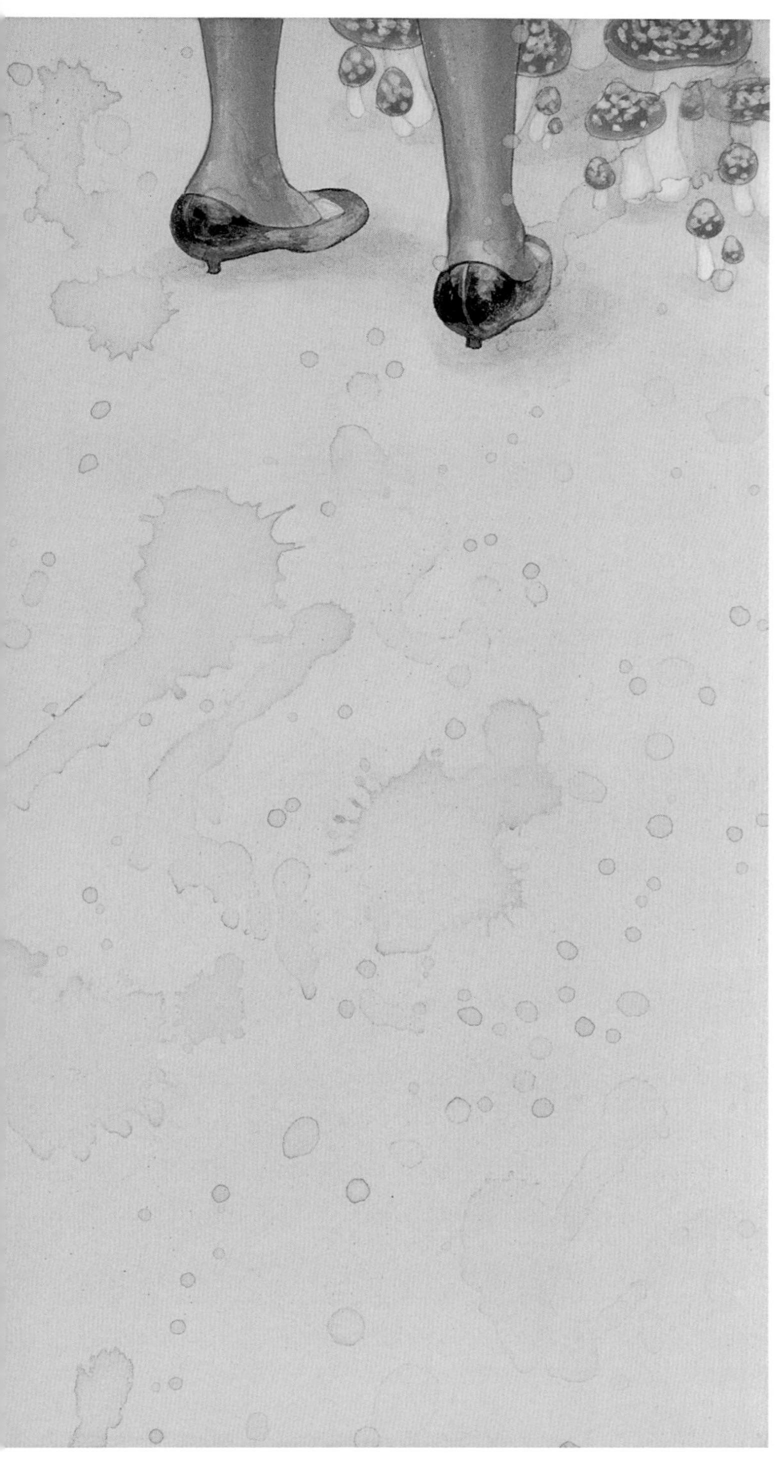

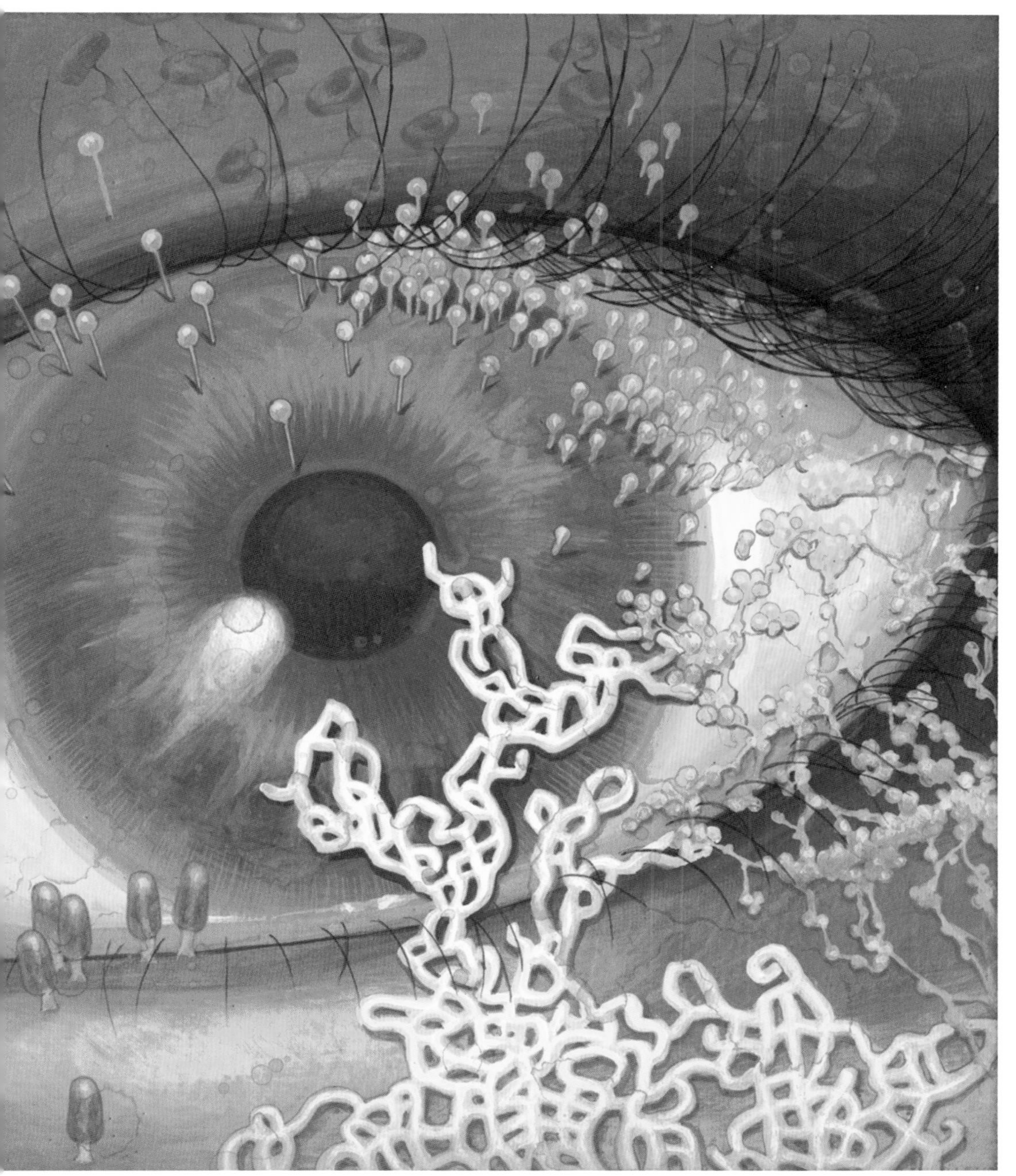

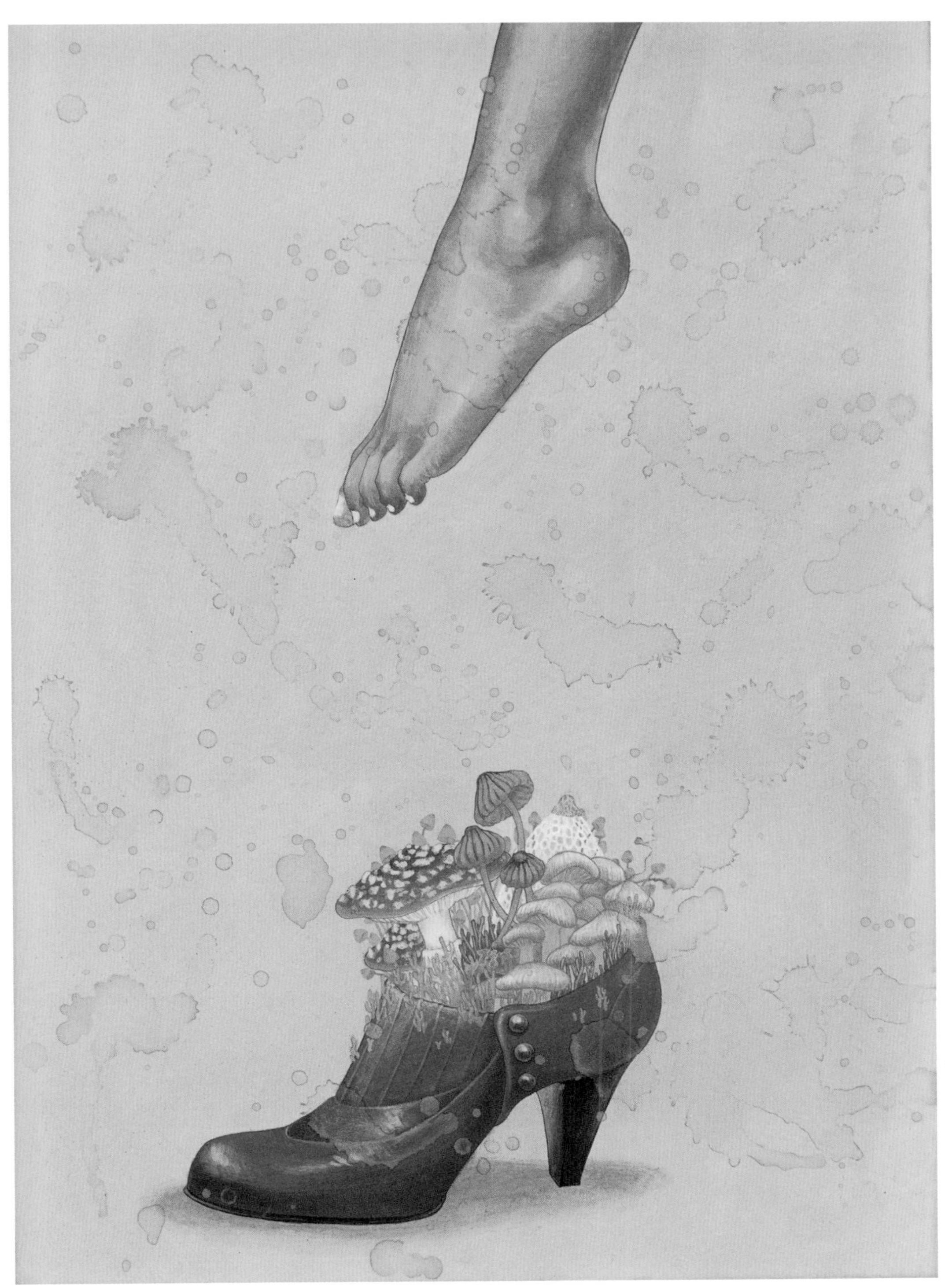

EMMA WHITELAW

ALLYN HOWARD

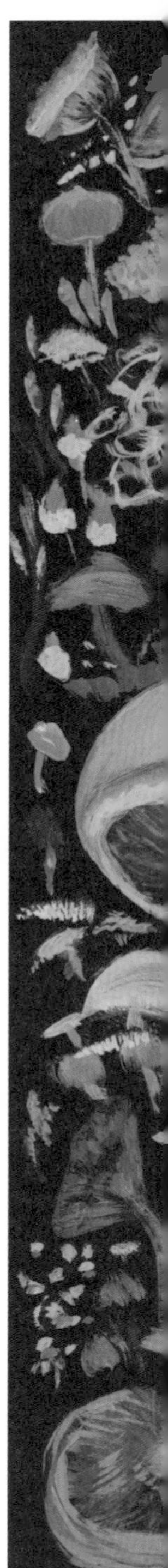

SERGEY BLOKH

Blokh

Blokh

ALPINE AYITA

BECCA BOYCE

beccaboyce.com

Becca is a pattern designer and illustrator who specialises in distinctive watercolour paintings inspired by her memories of her childhood in the English countryside, as well as her time spent in her kitchen garden. She creates packaging that is too nice not to save, stationery that is treasured, and textiles that breathe new life into the home.

074 BIRCH BOLETE LECCINUM SCABRUM
Watercolours, Paper
140 x 190 mm

075 FLY AGARIC AMANITA MUSCARIA
Watercolours, Paper
220 x 230 mm

076 WOOD BLEWITS AND PINE, FROM THE SERIES EDIBLE MUSHROOMS AND WHERE TO FIND THEM
Watercolours, Paper
670 x 950 mm

077 RUSSULAS AND OAK, FROM THE SERIES EDIBLE MUSHROOMS AND WHERE TO FIND THEM
Watercolours, Paper
670 x 950 mm

078 PARROT WAX CAPS AND MOSS, FROM THE SERIES EDIBLE MUSHROOMS AND WHERE TO FIND THEM
Watercolours, Paper
670 x 950 mm

079 INDIGO MILK CAP AND JUNIPER, FROM THE SERIES EDIBLE MUSHROOMS AND WHERE TO FIND THEM
Watercolours, Paper
670 x 950 mm

080 CANDY APPLE BOLETE EXSUDOPORUS FROSTII
Watercolours, Paper
240 x 280 mm

081 FUNGI RAINBOW
Watercolours, Paper
704 x 1000 mm

AMY ROSS

amyross.com

Boston-based artist Amy Ross uses collage to morph together human legs and mushroom caps to create fantastical hybrids. Her work also speaks to the interconnectedness of all life and is fueled by a deep reverence for the natural world. Amy's work has been exhibited in galleries throughout the country and is held in numerous private and public collections.

082 AMANITAS
Collage, Paper
229 x 178 mm

083 MORPHED MULTITUDE
Collage, Paper
762 x 559 mm

084 / 085 SHROOM IN REPOSE
Collage, Paper
216 x 280 mm

086 WALKING SHROOM
Collage, Paper
280 x 216 mm

087 LADYSHROOM
Collage, Paper
254 x 203 mm

088 / 089 FAIRY RING
Collage, Paper
559 x 762 mm

CECI LAM

behance.net/ceciilam

Ceci is an illustrator and animator based in Hong Kong. She graduated from Hong Kong Polytechnic University, but her passion lies in painting, drawing, and handcrafting. She loves to travel, and her images feature landscapes and people on her journey.

090 / 097 CHRISTMAS PREPARATION
Digital
210 x 297 mm

098 / 099 WALKING IN THE BOTANICAL GARDEN
Digital
297 x 420 mm

100 / 101 MISS MUSHY DAILY
Digital
297 x 420 mm

102 / 105 LAURA'S HOLIDAY
Digital
297 x 420 mm

DEANNE CHEUK

deannecheuk.com

Deanne Cheuk is a New York-based artist and creative director. She has been commissioned by Apple, Chanel, Essie, Henri Bendel, Levi's, Netflix, Converse, Uniqlo and The New York Times Magazine for her creative direction, design and typography. Her first book is called Mushroom Girls Virus.

106 / 109 RED CAP GIRLS SERIES, PART 01

MUSHROOM IN A TEA CUP 02

RED CAP GIRLS SERIES, PART 03
Oil Paint, Canvas
305 x 305mm

110 MUSHROOM VIRUS PEACETIME LUXURY BROWN EDIBLE
Digital
445 x 400mm

111 MUSHROOM VIRUS PEACETIME LUXURY PURPLE
Digital
476 x 400mm

112 UNDERSIDED 02
Oil Paint, Canvas
762 x 450mm

113 UNDERSIDED 03
Oil Paint, Canvas
813 x 635mm

JIAYUE LI

jiayue.li

Jiayue is an artist, illustrator, and graphic designer from Chengdu. With elements inspired by nature, music, and books, her art focuses on women's empowerment and mysticism. She graduated from Tongji University and has an MFA in Design from the School of Visual Arts in New York. Her clients include The New Yorker-, Vogue Singapore, and Google to name a few.

114 THE MUSHROOM BOX
Colour Pencil
195 x 245 mm

115 THRIVE
Colour Pencil
195 x 245 mm

116 FUNGI FAIRY
Colour Pencil
195 x 245 mm

118 / 119 THE POD FOR ANATOMY
Colour Pencil
305 x 215 mm

EMMA BLACK

emma-black.co.uk

Emma is a British visual artist and freelance illustrator. The unknown, whether an aspect of the physical world or a limitation of the human mind, is the main starting point for her work. Using mainly traditional media and autobiographical themes, Emma's practice explores notions of The Uncanny, the human subconscious, and our relationship to death and the natural world.

120 DREAM OF THE WITHERING FOREST
Oil Paint, Cradled Wood
203 x 254 mm

121 FORGOTTEN IS THE BLESSING
Oil Paint, Board
127 x 177 mm

122 THE DISSOLUTION OF MEMORY
Oil Paint, Cradled Wood
406 x 508 mm

123 BEAUTY IS BANKRUPT
Oil Paint, Cradled Wood
203 x 254 mm

124 HIDE IN THE DREAM
Oil Paint, Cradled Wood
304 x 406 mm

125 PAPERCUT
Oil Paint, Cradled Wood
279 x 355 mm

126 THE HARVEST
Oil Paint, Cradled Wood
304 x 406 mm

127 NO ONE KNOWS
Oil Paint, Cradled Wood
203 x 254 mm

FUCO UEDA

fucoueda.com

Born in 1979, Fuco Ueda graduated from Tokyo Polytechnic University and currently resides in Tokyo. She has held various solo and group exhibitions in various countries and published her art book "LUCID DREAM" in 2011.

128 SMALL FRIEND 3
Acrylic, Shell White, Canvas
100 mm Diameter

129 SYMBIOSIS "TOADSTOOL"
Acrylic, Shell White, Canvas
652 x 803 mm

130 / 131 THEY WELCOMED 2
Acrylic, Shell White, Canvas
183 x 257 mm

132 / 133 SYMBIOSIS4 SLIME MOULD
Acrylic, Shell White, Canvas
158 x 227 mm

134 A BEAUTIFUL LIGHTNING
Acrylic, Wood
420 x 420 mm

135 THEY WELCOMED 1
Acrylic, Shell White, Canvas
257 x 183 mm

EMMA WHITELAW

emmawhitelaw.com.au

Emma Whitelaw is a multidisciplinary artist specialising in illustration and fine art. Her work is bold, vibrant and colourful, and her subject matter primarily focuses on the natural world, particularly plants, birds, and insects. Emma enjoys multiple styles and flows between highly-detailed illustrations, to flat bold graphic style paintings, featuring intricate line work and geometric patterns.

136 GARDEN OF EDEN
Acrylic, Gold Foil, Stretched Canvas
1000 x 1000 mm

137 PEACHY MUSHROOM
Acrylic, Archival Paper
56 x 76 mm

138 GOLDEN ARCHES
Acrylic, Archival Paper
56 x 76 mm

139 MIDNIGHT MUSHROOMS
Acrylic, Archival Paper
56 x 76 mm

140 AUTUMN MUSHROOMS
Digital
210 x 297 mm

141 PINK AND BLUE MUSHROOMS
Digital
210 x 297 mm

ALLYN HOWARD

allynhoward.com

Allyn Howard is a Brooklyn-based painter with a BFA from Virginia Commonwealth University and a Master of Arts degree from New York University. She worked as a scenic artist in film and television and has created murals for residential and commercial sites. Her first children's picture book was released in 2022, and she is currently working on her second book.

142 PINK MUSHROOMS
Acrylic Paint, Wood Panel
254 x 254 mm

143 FUNGI FUN
Acrylic Paint, Wood Panel
457.2 x 457.2 mm

144 / 145 MUSHROOMLAND
Acrylic Paint, Wood Panel
254 x 254 mm

SERGEY BLOKH

instagram.com/blokh_sergey

Born in Volgograd in 1984, Sergey is not simply an artist, but also a symbolist and magician. He enjoys combining the incongruous and giving ordinary things a magical appeal. He graduated from the Volgograd State Institute of Arts and Culture in 2010.

146 TURQUOISE
Acrylic, Canvas
90 x 80 mm

147 SMOKE
Acrylic, Canvas
90 x 80 mm

148 LOVE IS LOVE
Acrylic, Canvas
90 mm Diameter

148 LITTLE WORLD
Acrylic, Canvas
100 mm Diameter

149 BOHO
Acrylic, Canvas
100 x 160 mm

150 / 151 EXIT 2
Acrylic, Canvas
100 x 80 mm

ALPINE AYITA

alpineayita.com

Created by Helen Smyth, Alpine Ayita's work resides predominantly in the natural world. Helen seeks to highlight the importance of biodiversity and to explore the relationship that humankind holds with the rest of nature and the effects that human activity has on wild spaces. She hopes for her work to bring about a sense of wonder in our living world.

152 FLY AGARIC AND BOLETE
Watercolours, Paper
210 x 297 mm

153 WOOD BLEWITT
Watercolours, Gouache, Paper
230 x 310 mm

154 WITHIN REACH
Watercolours, Paper
230 x 310 mm

155 TREAD SOFTLY
Watercolours, Paper
230 x 310mm

156 GOLIATH BEETLE AND LICHEN
Watercolours, Paper
230 x 310 mm

157 MIDSUMMER NIGHT
Watercolours, Gouache, Paper
230 x 310 mm

JAMES BARKER

RHIAN DAVIE ILLUSTRATION

RITA GOULD

SUNDRA ART

SELCHA UNI

ROMMY GONZÁLEZ

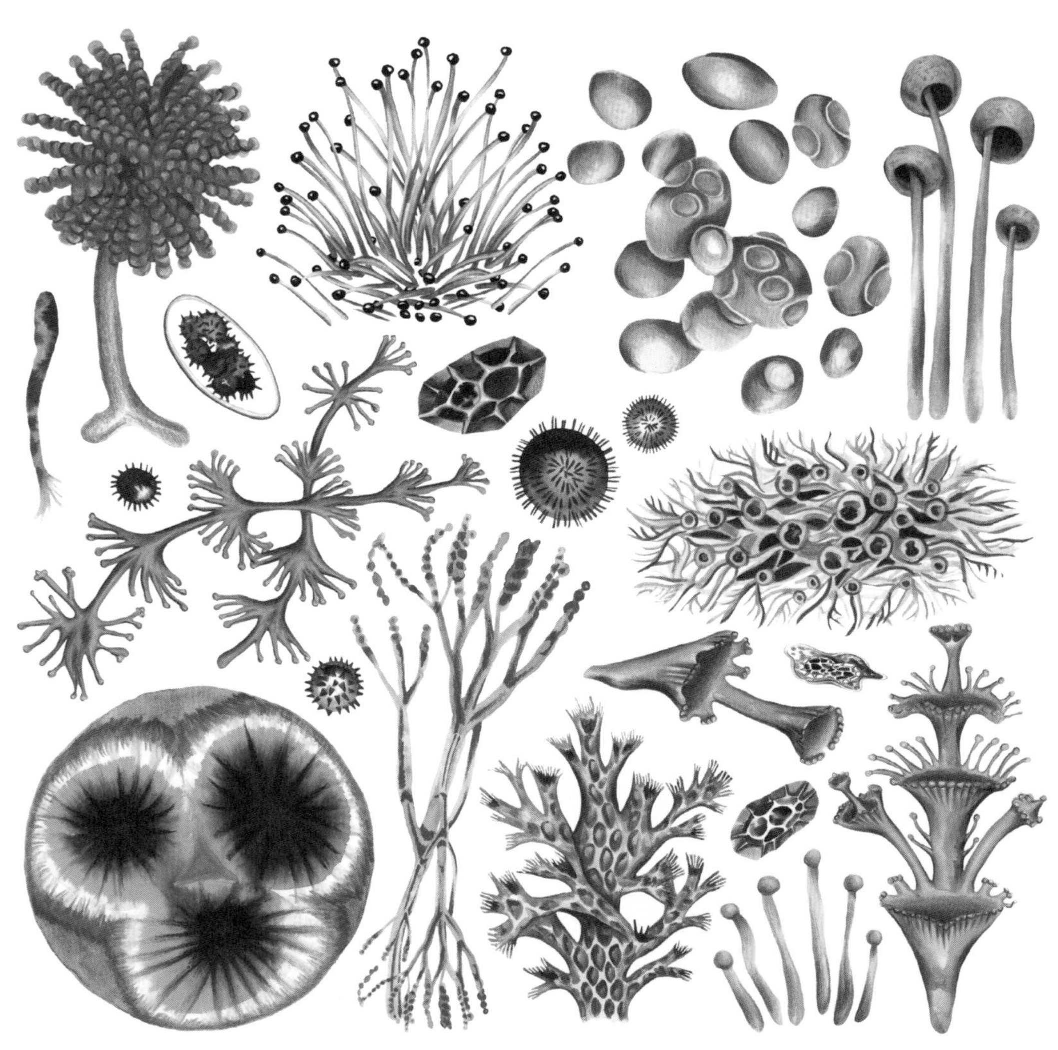

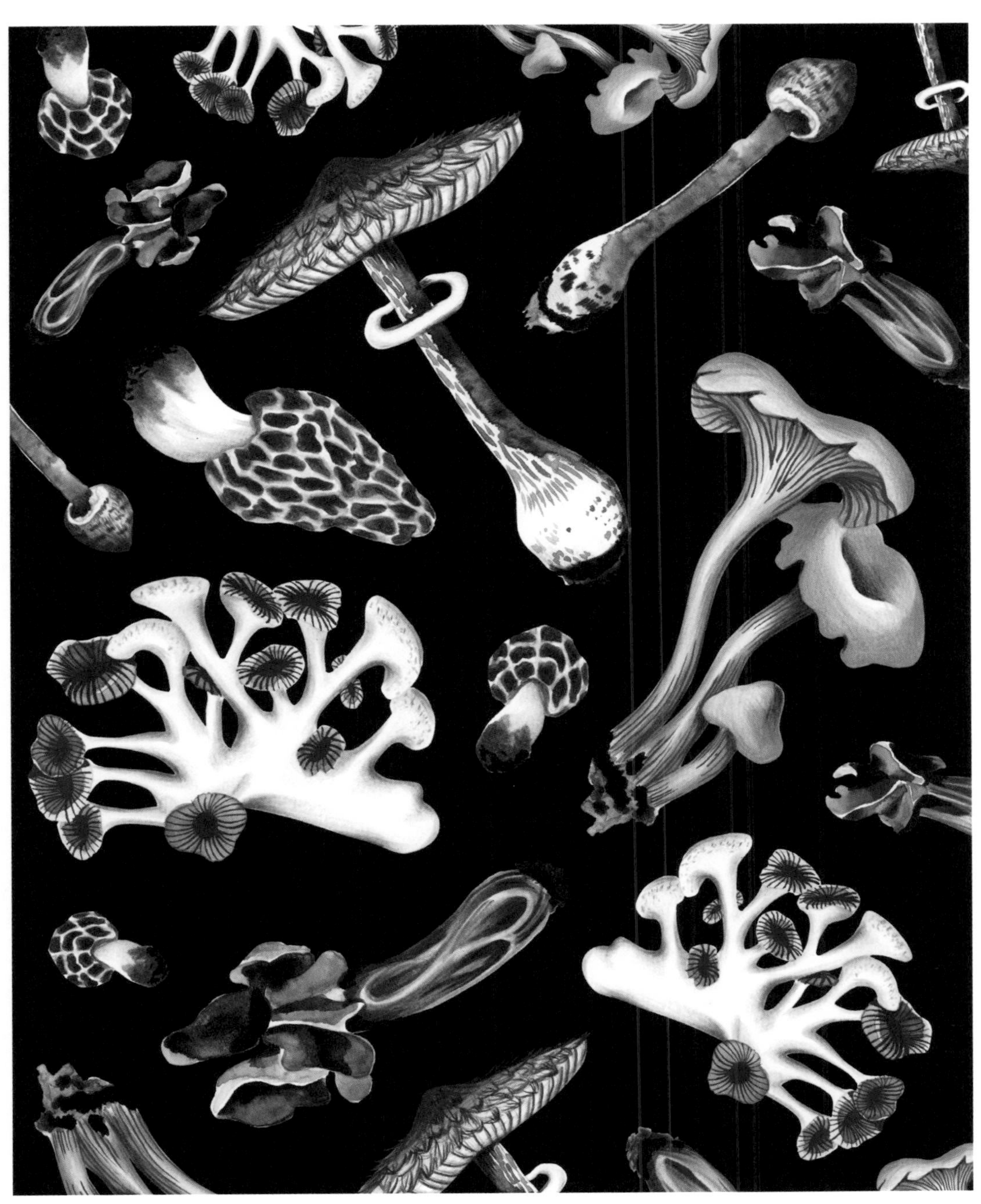

ELIZAVETA VOLGINA

EPISODIC DRAWING

Overnight, very
Whitely, discreetly,
Very quietly
Our toes, our noses
Take hold on the loam,
Acquire the air.
Nobody sees us,
Stops us, betrays us;
The small grains make room.

Excerpt from 'Mushrooms'
by Sylvia Plath

ROSA DE WEERD

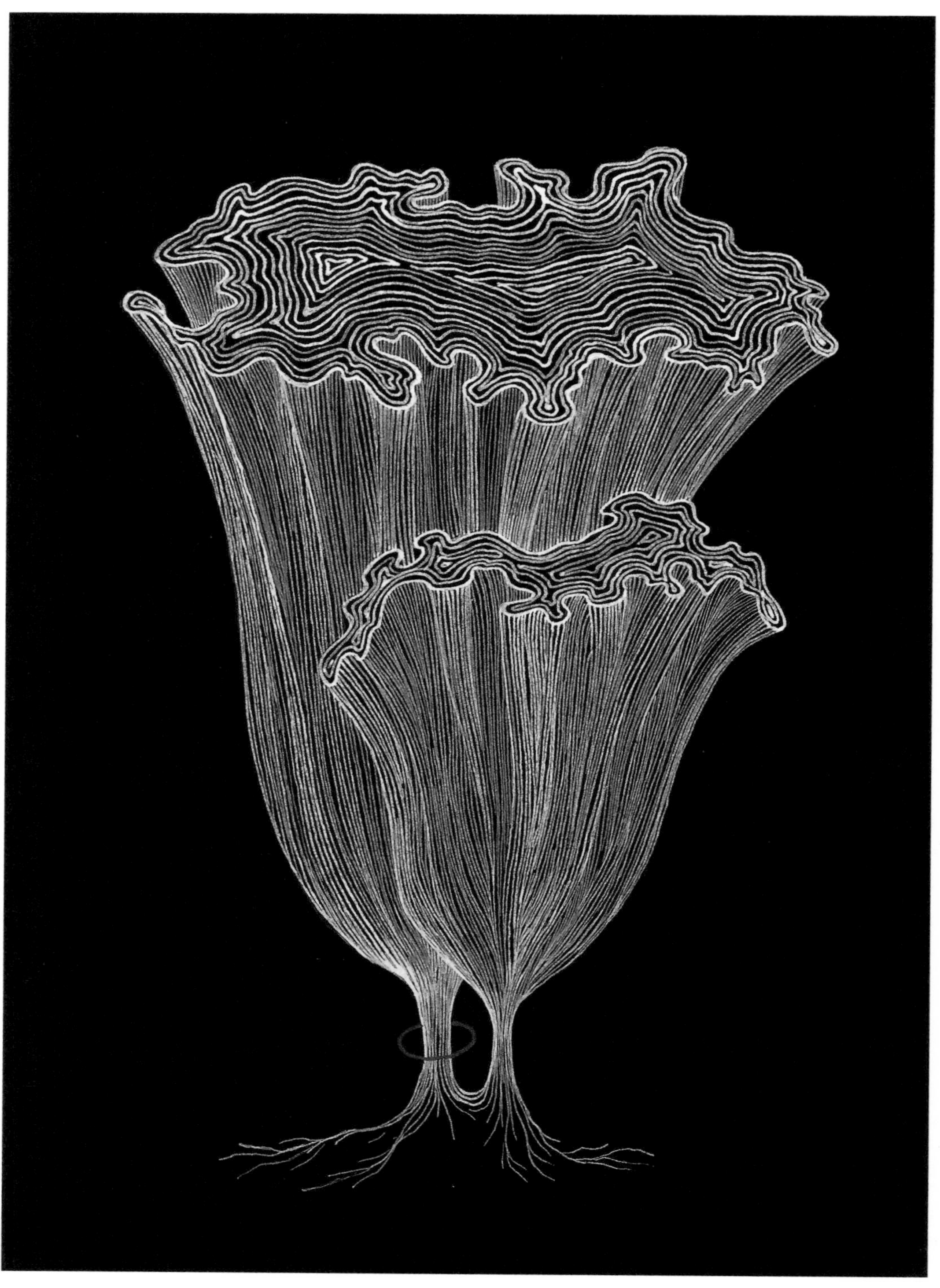

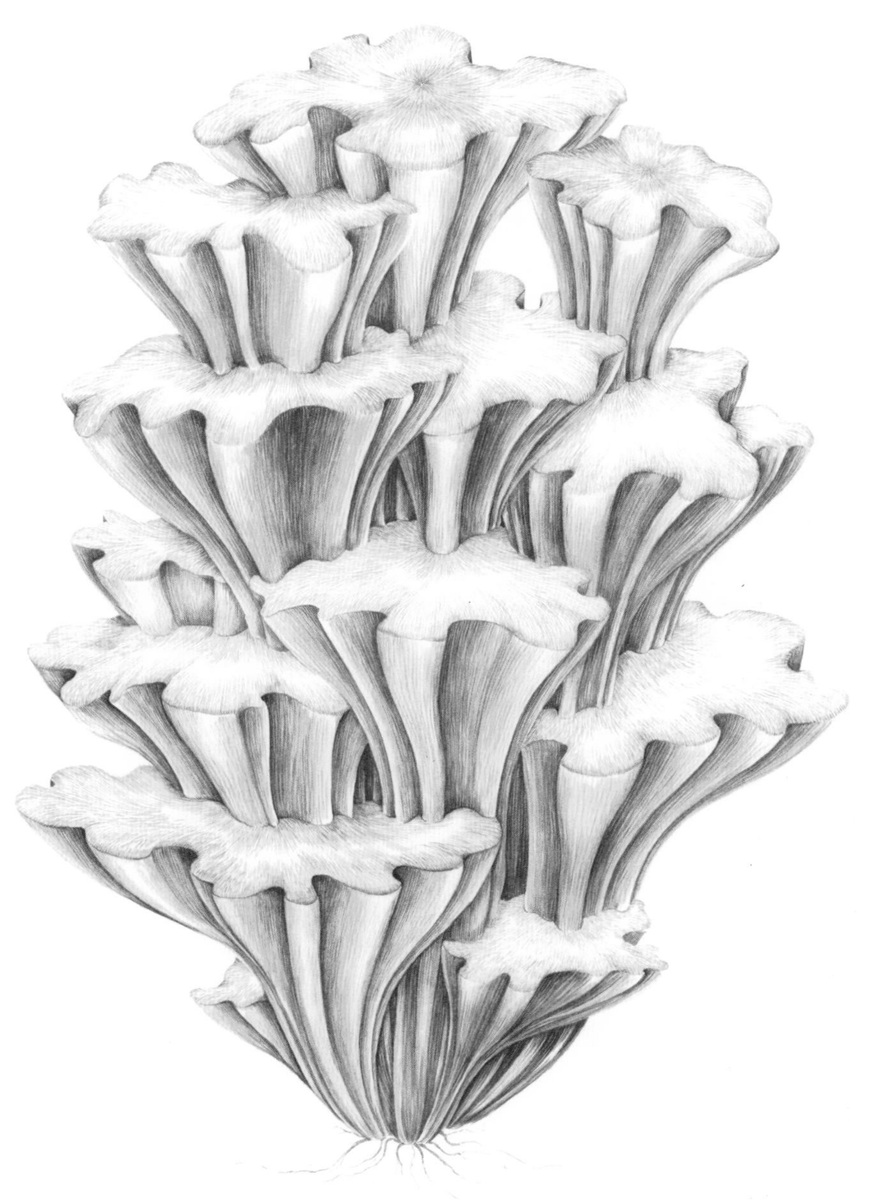

JAMES BARKER

james-barker.com

James is an illustrator based in London. He creates vibrant and quirky drawings inspired by nature and natural history whilst running his own label producing a range of witty illustration-led products.

162 FLY AGARIC
Colour Pencil, Digital
210 x 297 mm

163 ANISEED FUNNEL
Colour Pencil, Digital
210 x 297 mm

164 CHROOGOMPHUS
Colour Pencil, Digital
210 x 297 mm

165 SCALYHEAD
Colour Pencil, Digital
210 x 297 mm

166 SATAN'S BOLETE
Colour Pencil, Digital
210 x 297 mm

167 PINK DOMECAP
Colour Pencil, Digital
210 x 297 mm

168 SHAGGY INK CAP
Colour Pencil, Digital
210 x 297 mm

169 MARASMIUS
Colour Pencil, Digital
210 x 297 mm

170 MUSHROOM KINGDOM
Colour Pencil, Digital
297 x 420 mm

171 MUSHROOMS
Colour Pencil, Digital
297 x 420 mm

RHIAN DAVIE ILLUSTRATION

rhiandavie.com

Rhian Davie is a digital illustrator from South Wales. She creates work inspired by flora and fauna and the natural world, as well as being influenced by old botanical and animal illustrations. She often creates illustrations that include groups of natural history subjects or curiosities as she enjoys researching the beauty of nature.

172 RUSSULA EMETICA
Digital
210 x 297 mm

173 RUSSULA MUSHROOMS
Digital
210 x 297 mm

174 APRIL MUSHROOMS
Digital
210 x 297 mm

175 VERDIGRIS AGARIC
Digital
210 x 297 mm

176 INEDIBLE POISONOUS MUSHROOMS
Digital
210 x 297 mm

177 AMANITA MUSHROOMS
Digital
210 x 297 mm

178 POISONOUS MUSHROOMS
Digital
210 x 297 mm

179 BRITISH MUSHROOMS STUDY
Digital
210 x 297 mm

180 MUSHROOM GROUP
Digital
210 x 297 mm

181 MUSHROOMS AND FUNGI OF BRITAIN
Digital
210 x 297 mm

RITA GOULD

ritagould.com

Rita is a Russian independent artist and illustrator who lives in the UK. She created mostly nature related products inspired by her childhood memories, love for insects and things seen in gardens or in the wild. Mesmerised by the endless beauty of forests, rivers, gardens and its creatures, she replicates them using watercolours, gouache, and adds finishing details digitally.

182 BADGER
Watercolours, Gouache
210 x 297 mm

183 / 184 AUTUMN FORAGING
Watercolours, Digital
297 x 420 mm

185 AUTUMN FORAGING
Watercolours
297 x 420 mm

SUNDRA ART

sundra.art

Sundra Art was created by Aleksandra Smirnova, who as a child spent every summer in Siberian nature watching herbs, flowers, mushrooms, insects, and animals. She made many plein-air sketches and continued to draw all aspects of nature while paying attention to its details. She is always happy to see portraits of her tiny friends in different part of the world.

186 AUTUMN WILD NATURE
Watercolours, Paper
728 x 514 mm

187 AUTUMN WILD NATURE SET
Watercolours, Paper, Digital
472.4 x 662.1 mm

188 RED COLOURS IN SUMMER NATURE
Watercolours, Paper, Digital
818.2 x 593 mm

188 WHITE COLOURS IN SUMMER NATURE
Watercolours, Paper, Digital
818.2 x 593 mm

189 YELLOW COLOURS IN SUMMER NATURE
Watercolours, Paper, Digital
806 x 620.7 mm

189 SUMMER NATURE
Watercolours, Paper, Digital
818.2 x 593 mm

SELCHA UNI

instagram.com/selchauni

Selcha Uni is an independent Russian illustrator who is inspired by the textures of the forest, the scent of the steppes, and the voices of the sea.

190 MUSHROOM FOREST
Digital
280 x 280 mm

191 AUTUMN
Digital
280 x 280 mm

192 AMANITA
Digital
280 x 280 mm

193 BIRDS GARDEN
Digital
280 x 280 mm

ROMMY GONZÁLEZ

rommygonzalez.com

Rommy González is a Chilean visual artist based in Berlin since 2014 with a background in design and art direction. Inspired by botanical and scientific illustration, she plays around with fantasy and reality, creating imaginary landscapes. Her work ranges from illustrations, paintings, videos, performances, and surface design to urban art.

194 BASIDIOMYCETES AND SPORES (Funghiversum)
Mixed Media, Pencil, Watercolours, Ink, Gouache
297 x 420 mm
Special Credits: Katja Tannert, Angela Hundsdorfer

195 ASCOMYCETES AND SPORES (Funghiversum)
Mixed Media, Pencil, Watercolours, Ink, Gouache
297 x 420 mm
Special Credits: Katja Tannert, Angela Hundsdorfer

196 MICROFUNGUS, LICHENS AND SPORES (Funghiversum)
Mixed Media, Pencil, Watercolours, Ink, Gouache
297 x 420 mm
Special Credits: Katja Tannert, Angela Hundsdorfer

197 MUSHROOM COMPOSITION FINAL
Mixed Media, Pencil, Watercolours, Ink, Gouache
297 x 420 mm

198 FUNGHIVERSUM (Funghiversum)
Mixed Media, Pencil, Watercolours, Ink, Gouache, Digital
210 x 297 mm
Special Credits: Katja Tannert, Angela Hundsdorfer

199 FUNGISERIES BLACK
Mixed Media, Pencil, Watercolours, Ink, Gouache, Digital
297 x 420 mm

ELIZAVETA VOLGINA

instagram.com/botanicolors

Elizaveta was born in Saint-Petersburg and graduated form the Repin Academy of Arts in 2014. She works mainly in watercolour and is inspired by her childhood summers spent in nature. She is fascinated by insects and plants, and loves to capture their tiny world in harmony. In 2021, she took part in three exhibitions about botanical art in Saint-Petersburg, London, and Moscow respectively.

200 AMANITA COMPOSITION
Watercolours, White Tempera
299 x 220 mm

201 AMANITA MUSCARIA AND THE TOAD
Watercolours, White Tempera
176 x 224 mm

202 AMANITA MUSCARIA AND THE LITTLE FROG
Watercolours, White Tempera
251 x 347 mm

203 RED FLY AGARIC AND LARVA
Watercolours, White Tempera
236 x 353 mm

204 FOREST MEMORIES
Watercolours, White Tempera
329 x 255 mm

205 AMANITA GEMMATA
Watercolours, White Tempera
251 x 297 mm

206 / 207 CANTHARELLUS CIBARIUS
Watercolours, White Tempera
184 x 111 mm

EPISODIC DRAWING

episodic-drawing.com

Episodic Drawing is the work of artist Lea Yunk. In her heart, she believes that something magical happens at night. Her designs feature natural elements, symmetrical patterns, and a pop of colour on a dark background. Lea hopes her designs can bring some magical and calming qualities to people's hectic lives.

208 AUTUMN LIGHT UNDERWINGS
Digital
594 x 841 mm

209 LUNA AND EMERALD
Digital
610 x 610 mm

210 BLUE OYSTER
Digital
594 x 841 mm

ROSA DE WEERD

cargocollective.com/rosadeweerd

Rosa de Weerd is a Dutch illustrator and jewellery designer who focuses on flora and fauna. Her illustrations depict earthly subjects as well as otherworldly and peculiar plants, growing on undiscovered islands and faraway worlds. She also makes and paints jewellery boxes, which are perfect symbioses of all her passions combined: painting, history, and jewellery.

212 AURORA MUSHROOMS
210 x 149 mm

213 FOLIO SPECIMEN NO. 8
Watercolours, Gouache
148 x 210 mm

214 FOLIO SPECIMEN NO. 2
Watercolours, Gouache
148 x 210 mm

215 FOLIO SPECIMEN NO. 3
Watercolours, Gouache
148 x 210 mm

216 FOLIO SPECIMEN NO. 9
Watercolours, Gouache
148 x 210 mm

217 THE FOREST MUSHIES
Digital
148 x 210 mm

218 FOLIO SPECIMEN NO. 10
Watercolours, Gouache
148 x 210 mm

219 FOLIO SPECIMEN NO. 1
Watercolours, Gouache
148 x 210 mm

220 FOLIO SPECIMEN NO. 4
Watercolours, Gouache
148 x 210 mm

221 THE PINK PUSHROOMS
Watercolours, Gouache
420 x 290 mm

LÈA CHAILLAUD

Under a toadstool crept a wee Elf,
Out of the rain to shelter himself.
Under the toadstool, sound asleep,
Sat a big Dormouse all in a heap.
Trembled the wee Elf, frightened and yet
Fearing to fly away lest he get wet.
To the next shelter—maybe a mile!
Sudden the wee Elf smiled a wee smile.
Tugged till the toadstool toppled in two.
Holding it over him, gaily he flew.
Soon he was safe home, dry as could be.
Soon woke the Dormouse—"Good gracious me!
"Where is my toadstool?" loud he lamented.
—And that's how umbrellas first were invented.

'The Elf and The Dormouse'
by Oliver Herford

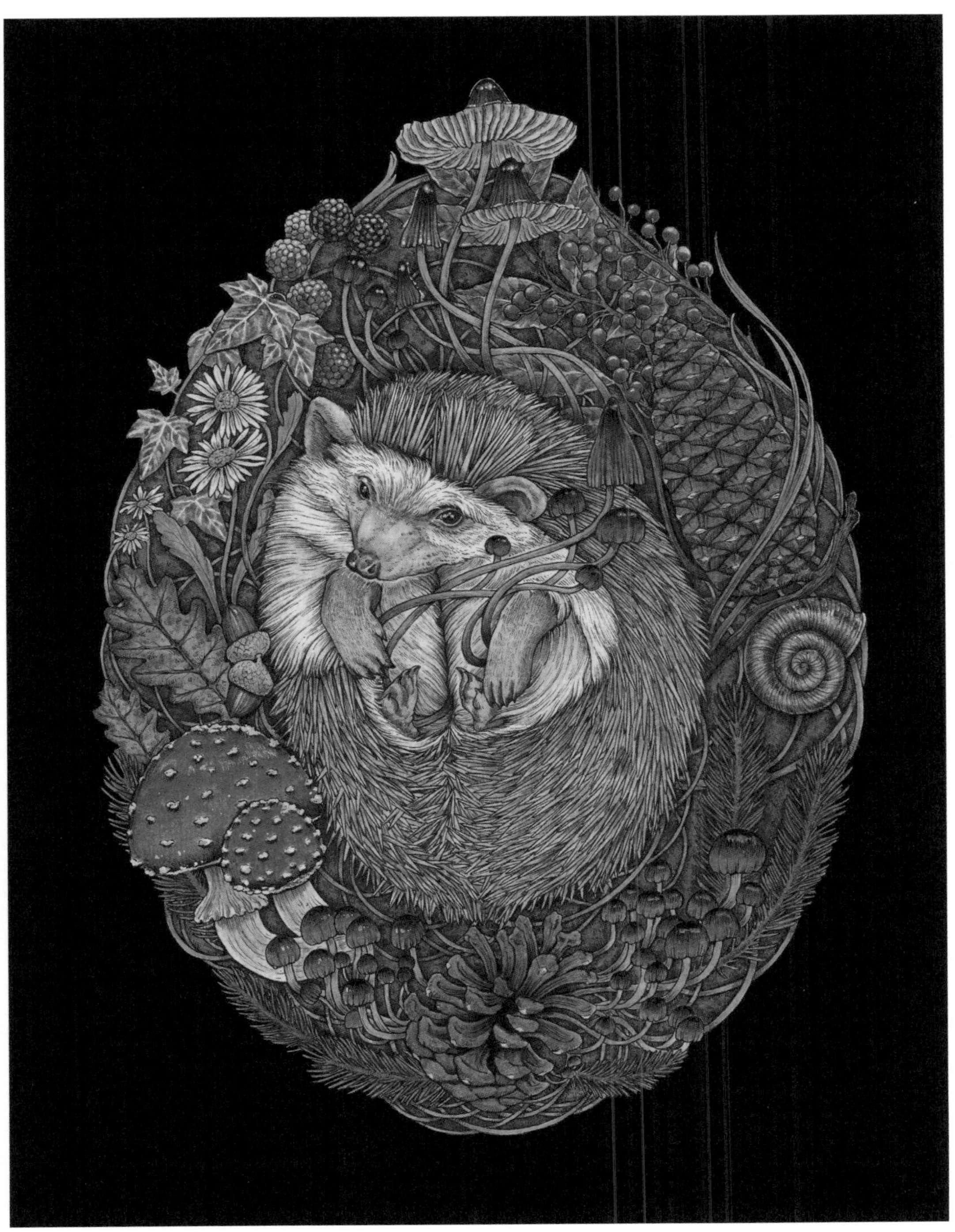

BEX PARKIN

TIFFANY BOZIC

KIT MIZERES

ALEJANDRO PASQUALE

All these years I overlooked them in the
racket of the rest, this
symbiotic splash of plant and fungus feeding
on rock, on sun, a little moisture, air —
tiny acid-factories dissolving
salt from living rocks and
eating them.

Here they are, blooming!
Trail rock, talus and scree, all dusted with it:
rust, ivory, brilliant yellow-green, and
cliffs like murals!
Huge panels streaked and patched, quietly
with shooting-stars and lupine at the base.

Excerpt from 'Springtime in the Rockies, Lichen'
by Lew Welch

ELIZABETH ENGLAND

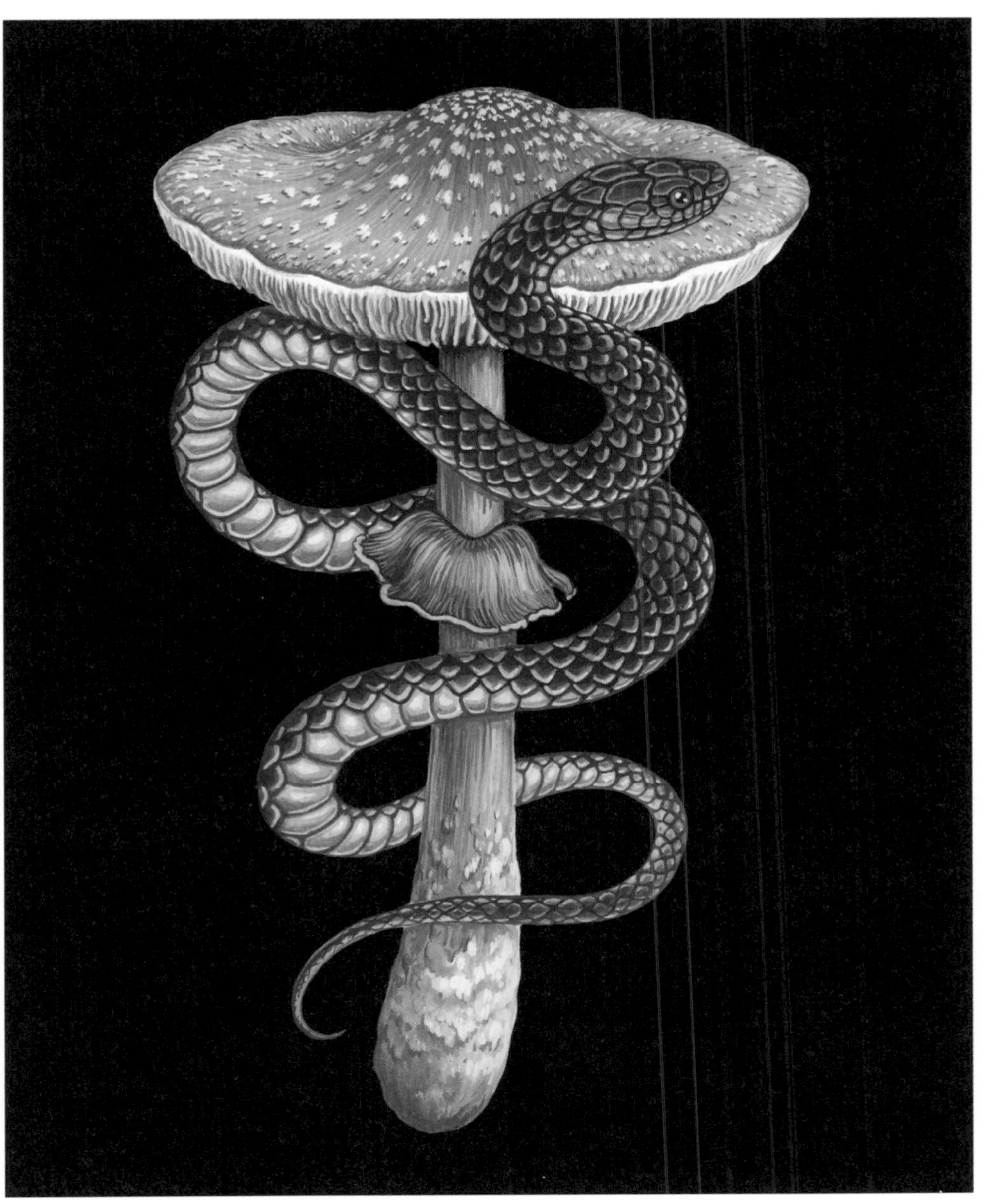

DONNA KATY JONES

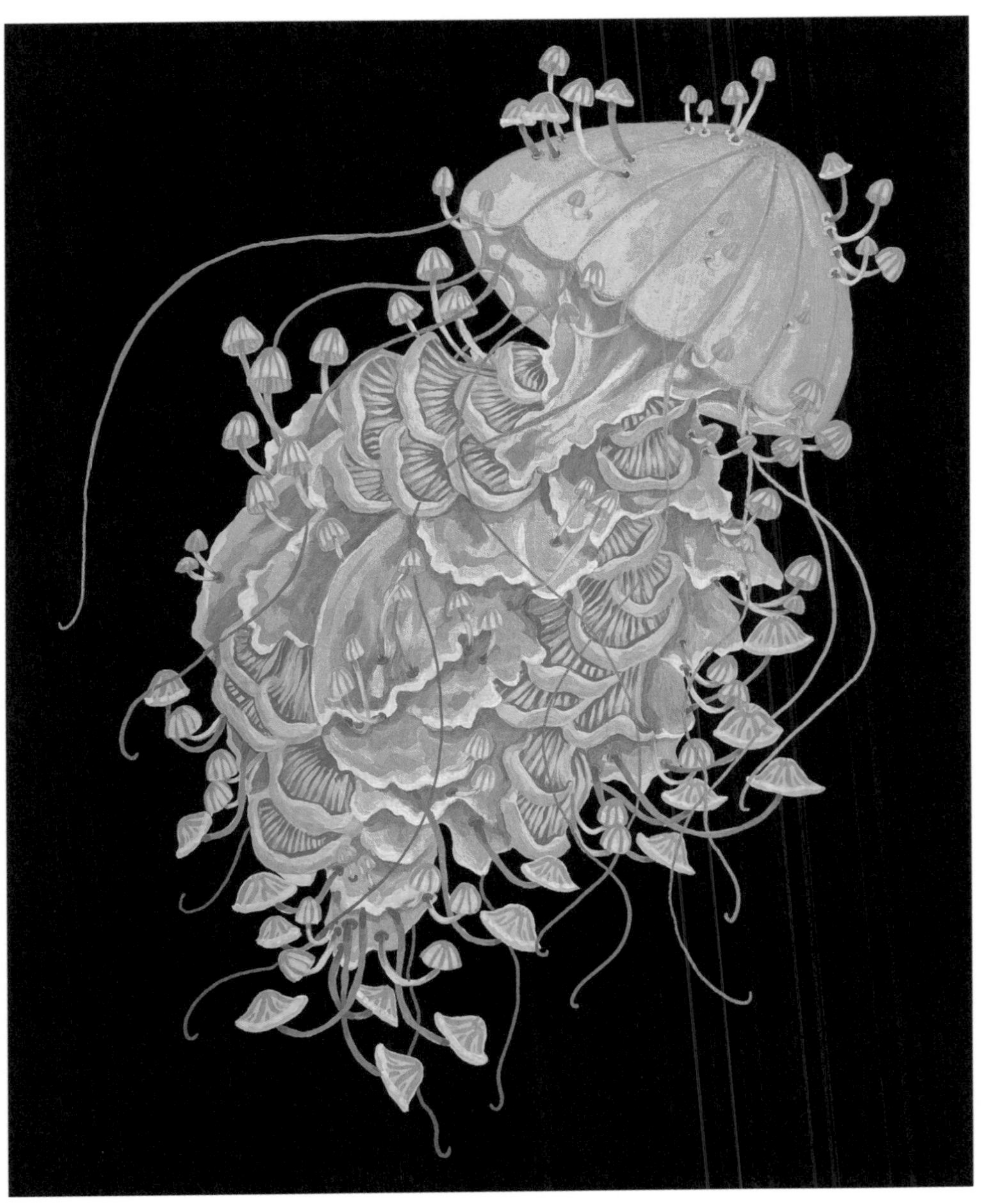

NADZEYA MAKEYEVA

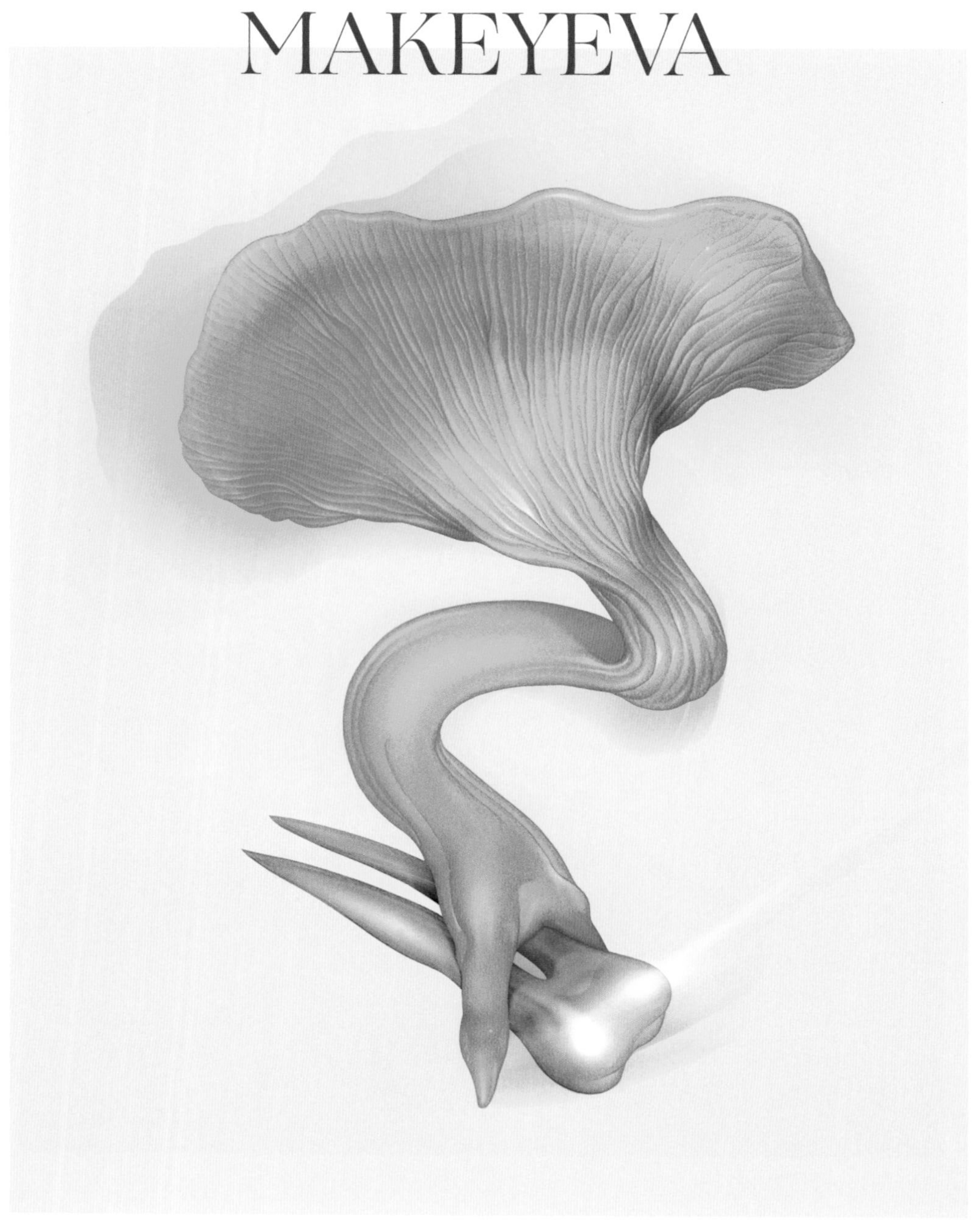

SILVER FRANCIS

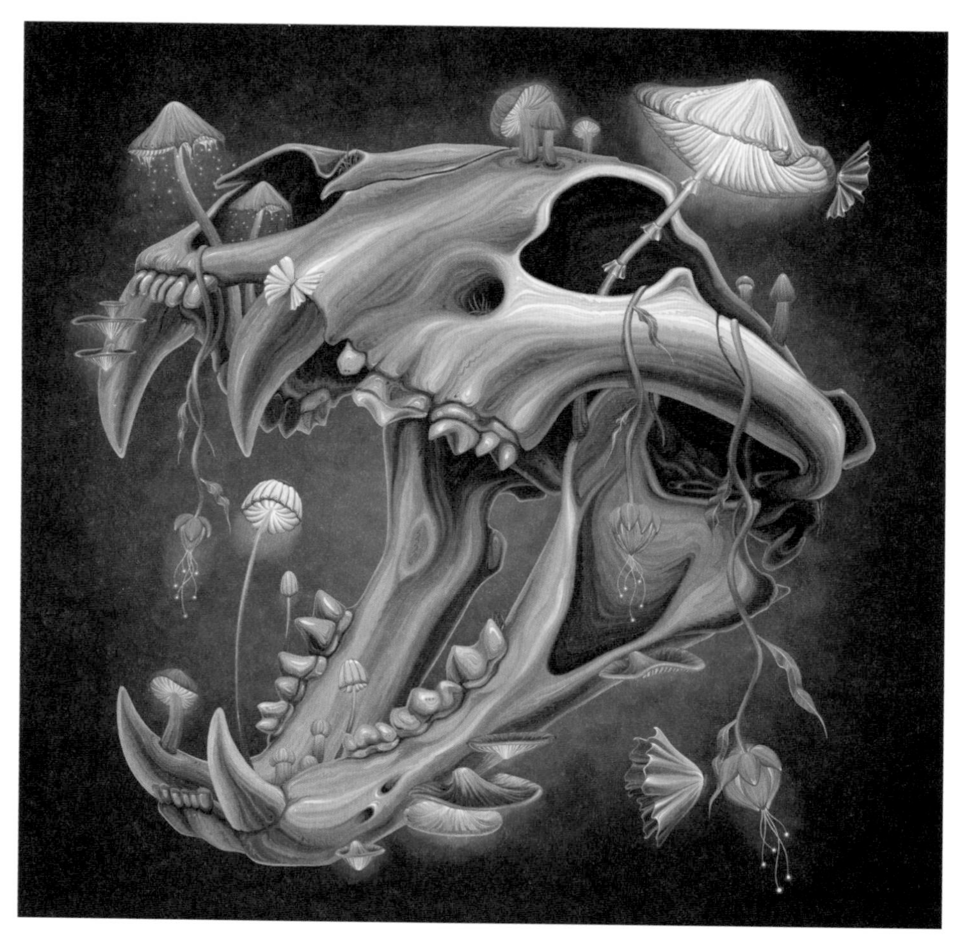

NICK LIEFHEBBER

L&W STUDIO

LÉA CHAILLAUD

leachaillaud.com

Léa Chaillaud is a French watercolour artist whose work revolves around the natural world and the representation of the fauna and flora of Europe, with a slight hint of fantasy. Using ink pens and watercolours, Léa creates intricate illustrations that take inspiration from a variety of folklore and fairy tales, as well as botanical illustrations and wildlife photography.

226 HEART OF THE FOREST
Watercolours, Pen and Ink, Colour Pencil
500 x 650 mm

227 AWAY WITH THE FAIRIES
Watercolours, Pen, Ink
210 x 297 mm

228 / 229 ALL AS ONE
Watercolours, Pen, Ink
210 x 297 mm

231 THE TREE KEEPERS
Watercolours, Pen, Ink
210 x 297 mm

232 FOREST FRIENDS
Watercolours, Pen, Ink
210 x 297 mm

233 WHILE YOU SLEPT
Watercolours, Pen, Ink
210 x 297 mm

BEX PARKIN

bexparkin.co.uk

Bex Parkin hand-paints all her designs in either gouache or watercolour from her studio in Staffordshire. After completing a degree in art history and graphic design at Central Saint Martins. she worked in many art galleries in London. To her, nature is endlessly inspiring, with all her designs featuring plants, birds and animals.

234 THE SQUIRREL AND THE COAL TIT
Watercolours, Paper
297 x 297 mm

235 THE STRAWBERRY PATCH
Watercolours, Paper
210 x 297 mm

TIFFANY BOZIC

tiffanybozic.com

Tiffany Bozic's work evokes the tradition of tightly rendered nature illustration, which she explores with highly emotional, surreal metaphors. As nature is ever more subjugated by human impacts, Bozic corrects the balance sheet and creates beautiful, celebratory, and also difficult work that reveals the complexities of natural processes like death and decomposition percolate through pictures of otherwise shining life..

236 CURIOSITY
Acrylic, Maple Panel
609.6 x 609.6 mm

237 STIMULI
Acrylic, Maple Panel
914.4 x 609.6 mm

238 DIVERSITY
Acrylic, Maple Panel
304.8 x 304.8 mm

239 SALINITY
Acrylic, Maple Panel
914.4 x 1066.8 mm

240 / 241 FLORA AND FAWN
Acrylic, Maple Panel
558.8 x 787.4 mm

KIT MIZERES

instagram.com/kitmizeresart

Kit Mizeres is an American artist and illustrator who hailed from Ohio and graduated from the Columbus College of Art and Design in Illustration. Since then, she continues to collect and draw inspiration from her new and ever-changing surroundings. Her work often takes on a maximalist, dreamlike approach that heavily incorporates themes of folklore and personal mythology.

242 TOXIC TONGUE
Gouache, Wood Panel
127 x 179 mm

243 SILLY SLOTH
Oil Paint, Wood Panel
355 x 200 mm

244 ROUGH LANDING
Oil Paint, Wood Panel
152 x 152 mm

245 TEMPERANCE
Gouache, Wood Panel
152 x 152 mm

ALEJANDRO PASQUALE

alejandropasquale.com

Alejandro is a self-taught artist from Buenos Aires who studied Fine Art at the National Institute of Art. Alejandro has worked with multiple art galleries in Melbourne, Barcelona, New York, and London to name a few. He has also participated in several art fairs globally, and his art has been included in private collections worldwide.

246 AURUM (Marco museum collection, Buenos Aires)
Oil Paint, Canvas
950 x 820 mm

247 LA HORA DORADA (Private Collection, Sonoma)
Oil Paint, Canvas
1500 x 1150 mm

248 / 249 ESPORA
Oil Paint, Acrylic, Canvas
1150 x 1460 mm

250 PORTAL (Private collection, Toronto)
Oil Paint, Canvas
600 x 300 mm

251 LA PORCIÓN ÁUREA (Private collection, Buenos Aires)
Oil Paint, Canvas
1500 x 1300 mm

253 PUENTE (Private collection, Miami)
Oil Paint, Canvas
1400 x 1100 mm

ELIZABETH ENGLAND

elizabethengland.com

Born in Texas, Elizabeth earned her BFA in studio art in 2014. With a reverence for the divine in nature — she seeks communion with the spiritual and material worlds. Magical, dreamlike, and mystical concepts combine in otherwise naturalistic scenes, alongside lighthearted paintings and meticulous scientific illustrations.

254 VERDIGRIS AGARIC AND TOAD FRIEND
Gouache, Colour Pencil
150 x 225 mm

255 WOOD BLEWITT AND SNAIL FRIEND
Gouache, Colour Pencil
150 x 225 mm

256 MEDICINAL MUSHROOMS
Colour Pencil
280 x 355 mm

257 SHROOM OF ASCLEPIUS
Gouache
200 x 250 mm

258 OMPHALOTUS ILLUDENS
Oil Paint, Panel
300 x 300 mm

259 MAGIC MUSHROOMS
Watercolours
125 x 175 mm

DONNA KATY JONES

instagram.com/donnakatyjones

Donna Katy Jones is from the foothills of Yosemite and lives in Chicago. She is inspired by her roots in nature and paints with acrylic and watercolours.

260 KING SNAKE AND MUSHROOMS
Acrylic, Canvas
457 x 609 mm

261 BETA FISH AND MUSHROOMS
Acrylic, Canvas
228 x 609 mm

262 EGRET AND MUSHROOMS
Acrylic, Canvas
914 x 1219 mm

263 JELLYFISH AND MUSHROOMS
Acrylic, Canvas
609 x 914 mm

NADZEYA MAKEYEVA

nadzeya-makeyeva.com

Nadzeya Makeyeva is a multidisciplinary illustrator and artist who lives and works in San Francisco. She is a member of the Society of Illustrators of Los Angeles. Nadzeya is inspired to work with design-focused organisations to create editorial art, website graphics, posters, portraits, app visuals, covers, and characters

264 BUBBLE GUM MONSTERS: THE OYSTER FUNGI
Digital, Pencil, Paper
230 x 531 mm

265 THE EYED MUSHROOM
Digital, Pencil, Paper
423 x 531 mm

266 KIROVA ST.
Digital, Pencil, Paper
500 x 500 mm

267 THE AMANITA RABBIT
Digital, Pencil, Paper
195 x 279 mm

SILVER FRANCIS

silverfrancisartwork.com

Silver Francis is a full-time impressionist painter based out of Tuscaloosa. Over years of experimentation, she has developed a unique style of contemporary impressionism in which layered strokes of paint blend seamlessly into one another. Through her work, she explores themes such as creation and decay, death and rebirth, collapse and regeneration, and hope.

268 LYNX
Oil Paint, Canvas
914.4 x 914.4 mm

269 ALICE
Oil Paint, Canvas
609.6 x 1219.2 mm

270 NOVA
Oil Paint, Canvas
609.6 x 1219.2 mm

271 DEADLY GLOW
Oil Paint, Canvas
304.8 x 609.6 mm

NICK LIEFHEBBER

liefhebber.biz

Nick Liefhebber creates bold, fun and colourful illustrations. Both commissioned and his own screen and Riso prints. Inspired by patterns and rhythms, he uses the associative powers of shape and material to communicate at an intuitive level. His images are built like a collage of paper cuts, ink drawings, and computer-generated imperfections.

272 HORSES GALLOPING FULL SPEED THROUGH THE FOREST
Digital
182.1 x 136.5 mm

273 FLUORESCENT DAWN IN THE MICROBE FOREST
Digital
182 x 136.5 mm

274 / 275 PROCREATE 5 LAUNCH CAMPAIGN (Savage Interactive)
Digital
133 x 100 mm

L&W STUDIO

lw-art.com

L&W studio was formed by Lin Yu-Ching & Wei Hsing-Yu, an artist duo from Taiwan. With minds filled with whimsy, they create fantastic plants and peculiar creatures that escape the framework of reality and travel freely in an imaginary world. Their work also frequently explores the unknown and is a projection of reality, awaiting exploration in an intertwining cycle.

276 NAIVE MONSTER (Dynasty Gallery)
Mixed Media, Paper
400 x 550 mm

277 ROCK N' ROLL LAND OF LONELINESS (Dynasty Gallery)
Mixed Media, Paper
1600 x 1100 mm

278 THE STONE OF YESTERDAY (Dynasty Gallery)
Mixed Media, Paper
550 x 400 mm

279 PHANTOM LAKE (Dynasty Gallery)
Mixed Media, Paper
700 x 700 mm

280 / 281 EXCHANGING OF GIFTS (Dynasty Gallery)
Mixed Media, Paper
1100 x 800 mm

282 / 283 ORANGE ROCK N' ROLL (Dynasty Gallery)
Technical Pen, Paper
1100 x 2400 mm

ACKNOWLEDGEMENTS

We would like to specially thank all the artists and illustrators who are featured in this book for their significant contribution towards its compilation. We would also like to express our deepest gratitude to our producers for their invaluable advice and assistance throughout this project, as well as the many professionals in the creative industry who were generous with their insights, feedback, and time. To those whose input was not specifically credited or mentioned here, we also truly appreciate your support.

FUTURE EDITIONS

If you wish to participate in viction:ary's future projects and publications, please send your portfolio to: we@victionary.com